Learn Python Programming by Coding Retro Games

A Hands-On Python Course Inspired by 80s and 90s Classics

Kevin Wilson

Python Programming Retro Games

Copyright © 2025 Elluminet Press

This work is subject to copyright. All rights are reserved by the Publisher, whether the whole or part of the material is concerned, specifically the rights of translation, reprinting, reuse of illustrations, recitation, broadcasting, reproduction on microfilms or in any other physical way, and transmission or information storage and retrieval, electronic adaptation, computer software, or by similar or dissimilar methodology now known or hereafter developed. Exempted from this legal reservation are brief excerpts in connection with reviews or scholarly analysis or material supplied specifically for the purpose of being entered and executed on a computer system, for exclusive use by the purchaser of the work. Duplication of this publication or parts thereof is permitted only under the provisions of the Copyright Law of the Publisher's location, in its current version, and permission for use must always be obtained from the Publisher. Permissions for use may be obtained through Rights Link at the Copyright Clearance Centre. Violations are liable to prosecution under the respective Copyright Law.

Trademarked names, logos, and images may appear in this book. Rather than use a trademark symbol with every occurrence of a trademarked name, logo, or image we use the names, logos, and images only in an editorial fashion and to the benefit of the trademark owner, with no intention of infringement of the trademark.

The use in this publication of trade names, trademarks, service marks, and similar terms, even if they are not identified as such, is not to be taken as an expression of opinion as to whether or not they are subject to proprietary rights.

This book references classic video games, including Tetris, Pong, Super Mario, Breakout, Space Invaders, and various others, for educational and historical purposes. All trademarks, game titles, and intellectual properties mentioned remain the property of their respective owners. The projects featured in this book are original works developed for instructional purposes. They are inspired by classic games but are not affiliated with, endorsed by, or derived from any proprietary game source or trademark holder.

While the advice and information in this book are believed to be true and accurate at the date of publication, neither the authors nor the editors nor the publisher can accept any legal responsibility for any errors or omissions that may be made. The publisher makes no warranty, express or implied, with respect to the material contained herein.

Images used with permission. Wackerhausen, RainerKnäpper, KDS4444, monsitj, HLundgaard @ iStock. Mnyjhee @ Dreamstime. VIA Gallery from Hsintien, MikeRun, Danrok, Stockarch, Michael Gauthier, Luminescent Media / CC-BY-SA-3.0, 200 Degrees Pixabay, Rikitikitao | Dreamstime.com, VicFic2006

eBook versions and licenses are also available for most titles. Any supplementary material referenced by the author in this text is available to readers at

www.elluminetpress.com/resources

Table of Contents

About the Author 7
Acknowledgements 9
Getting Started 10
    Why Learn Game Programming? 11
    What is Python? 13
    Installing Python 13
        Install on Windows.. *13*
    Install on MacOS 17
    Install on Linux 18
    Introduction to Pygame... 19
    Install Pygame 21
    Setting up your Development Environment 22
        Code Editor vs IDE *22*
        Visual Studio Code (VS Code)................................. *23*
        IDLE.. *25*
    Organizing Your Projects.. 27
Intro to Python... 28
    Statements 29
    Reserved Words 30
    Indentation.. 30
    Comments 31
    Variables 33
    Arrays, Lists and Tuples 34
    Dictionaries 35
    Operators 36
        Arithmetic Operators.. *37*
        Comparison Operators.. *37*
        Logical Operators... *38*
        Assignment Operators *38*
    Conditional Statements 39
        The if Statement *39*
        Using if...else... *39*
        Adding More Conditions with elif *39*
        Indentation Matters *40*
    Match Statements.. 40
    Loops 41
        While Loops *42*

For Loops	*42*
Breaking Out of a Loop	*43*
Skipping a Turn in the Loop	*43*
Loops in Game Development	*43*
Functions	43
Functions with Parameters	44
Returning Values from Functions	44
Classes & Objects	45
Defining a Class & Adding Attributes	*45*
Adding Methods	*46*
Creating Objects	*47*
Why Use Classes in Games?	*47*
File Handling	48
Writing to a File	*49*
Reading from a File	*49*
Appending to a File	*49*
Real-World Game Example	*50*
Using Modules	50
Using Third Party Modules	*50*
Importing Libraries	*51*
Creating your Own	*52*
Exercises	52
Challenge	53

Game Windows & Loops 54

Creating a Game Window	55
What Is a Game Loop?	57
Challenge	60

Drawing to the Screen 62

Blitting Images	63
Drawing Shapes	65
Adding Text	66
Surfaces, Rects, and Coordinates	67
Using Colors	69
Challenge	71

Sprites & Movement 72

Creating Player & Enemy Objects	73
Keyboard Events in Pygame	75
Game Controllers	80
Collision Detection	84
Animations	88

  Challenge 90
Sound & Music.. 92
  Initializing the Mixer 93
  Loading and Playing Sound Effects 93
  Background Music.. 94
  Challenge 95
Simple Shooter 96
  Game Description 97
  Requirements 97
    Functional..98
    Non-Functional..98
  Assets...99
  Design..99
  Implementation 102
  Challenge 106
My Invaders Project 108
  Game Description 109
  Requirements 110
    Functional..110
    Non-Functional..110
  Assets... 111
  Analysis... 111
  Design & Implementation 112
    The Player...113
    The Bullet 114
    The Bomb..115
    The Enemy...116
    The Fleet 117
    Game State and Main Loop 121
Simple Platformer 126
  Game Description 127
  Requirements 128
    Functional..128
    Non-Functional..128
  Assets... 128
  Analysis... 129
  Designing the Level.. 131
  Design and Implementation 133
    Tile..133

Coin	*134*
Enemy	*135*
Player	*136*
Game State and Main Loop	*140*
Creating the Game State	*142*
Main Game Loop	*143*
Challenge	146
Brick Basher	**148**
Game Description	149
Requirements	149
Functional	*149*
Non-Functional	*150*
Analysis	150
Design and Implementation	152
Paddle	*152*
Ball	*153*
Brick	*154*
BrickField	*154*
Game State	*155*
Main Game Loop	*156*
Challenge	160
Going Beyond Pygame	**162**
Panda3D	163
Godot	164
Unity	165
Unreal Engine	166
Choosing Your Next Engine	167
Video Resources	**168**
Using the Videos	169
File Resources	170
Scanning the Codes	172
iPhone	*172*
Android	*173*
Glossary of Terms	**174**
Python Reference	**186**
Index	**192**

About the Author

With over 20 years' experience in the computer industry, Kevin Wilson has made a career out of technology and showing others how to use it. After earning a master's degree in computer science, software engineering, and multimedia systems, Kevin has held various positions in the IT industry including graphic & web design, programming, building & managing corporate networks, and IT support.

He serves as senior writer and director at Elluminet Press Ltd, he periodically teaches computer science at college, and works as an IT trainer in England while researching for his PhD. His books have become a valuable resource among the students in England, South Africa, Canada, and in the United States.

Kevin's motto is clear: "If you can't explain something simply, then you haven't understood it well enough." To that end, he has created the Exploring Tech Computing series, in which he breaks down complex technological subjects into smaller, easy-to-follow steps that students and ordinary computer users can put into practice.

You can contact Kevin using his email address:

office@elluminetpress.com

Acknowledgements

Thanks to all the staff at Luminescent Media & Elluminet Press for their passion, dedication and hard work in the preparation and production of this book.

To all my friends and family for their continued support and encouragement in all my writing projects.

To all my colleagues, students and testers who took the time to test procedures and offer feedback on the book

Finally thanks to you the reader for choosing this book. I hope it helps you gain a better understanding of Python Programming by having fun creating your own games.

Getting Started

Game development is one of the most engaging ways to learn computer programming. It combines logic, creativity, and real-time interaction, offering immediate feedback on the code you write. Unlike abstract programming exercises, games give your code a purpose — to move characters, generate levels, detect collisions, play sounds, and entertain players.

Chapter by chapter, we'll explore the ins and outs of Python with illustrations, worked examples, lab exercises and projects for you to complete yourself.

We've included all the source code for this chapter in the following repository:

elluminetpress.com/gamestarter

Have Fun!

Chapter 1: Getting Started

Why Learn Game Programming?

By writing games, you don't just learn how to code — you learn how to think like a developer: solving problems, analysing systems, and building well-structured solutions through planning, development, and testing. This process not only deepens your understanding of programming, but also teaches you how to design systems with clarity, purpose, and efficiency — essential skills for any software developer using any programming language.

This book draws inspiration from the early era of video games — spanning the late 1970s through the 1980s — a period defined by creative innovation within strict hardware limitations. With limited memory, low processing power, and basic graphics capabilities, developers focused on gameplay mechanics, challenge, and player interaction to create titles that remain influential to this day.

We'll create our own versions of classic games like Space Invaders, Breakout/Arkanoid, Pong, Platformers, and many others, as well as titles released on iconic machines such as the Atari 520STFM and Amiga 500.

Chapter 1: Getting Started

You won't need a retro console to follow along — we'll use Python and Pygame to recreate our own versions of some of these classics.

By studying and rebuilding these timeless classics, you'll learn how to use the Python language itself to write clear, effective, and well-structured code. You'll work with variables, conditionals (if/else), and loops (for and while) to control the flow of gameplay, and use functions with arguments to break code into logical, reusable blocks.

You'll define classes and objects to represent game entities like players, enemies, and projectiles using object-oriented programming principles.

To manage data, you'll use lists, dictionaries, tuples, and sets, giving you flexible ways to store and manipulate things like scores, inventory, or enemy patterns.

As your games grow, you'll learn to organize code into modules and packages, making your projects easier to manage and maintain.

You'll also implement error handling with try/except blocks to catch problems gracefully — like missing files or invalid inputs — and use file input and output to load levels or save game progress.

Along the way, you'll take advantage of powerful built-in Python modules such as random, time, and os to control game timing, generate unpredictable behavior, and interact with the file system.

You'll also gain insight into:

- Good programming practice and problem solving skills
- Efficient 2D collision and movement logic
- Game state handling and memory management
- Tight control loops and minimal latency
- How hardware constraints inspired smart design

Chapter 1: Getting Started

What is Python?

Python is a high-level programming language created by Guido van Rossum and first released in 1991. The name "Python" was inspired by Guido's love for the British comedy series "Monty Python's Flying Circus".

Python emphasizes code readability and aims to provide a clear and concise syntax, making it easier for programmers to express concepts and ideas in fewer lines of code compared to other programming languages. There is also a comprehensive library that provides a wide range of built in modules and functions for common programming tasks. This philosophy encourages the reuse of existing code and reduces the need for developers to rely heavily on third-party libraries for basic functionalities. Over the years, Python has attracted a large community of developers who contribute to its extensive ecosystem of third-party libraries and frameworks, further expanding its capabilities.

Python is designed to be a versatile language and is widely used in web development, data analysis, artificial intelligence, scientific computing, and automation.

Installing Python

In this section, we'll take a look at how to install the python interpreter and development environment.

Python 3 is the current and only supported version of the language, with new features and active updates. You can install Python on Windows, macOS, or Linux.

You can install python on Windows, Mac, or linux.

Install on Windows

In our lab, we're using windows workstations, so we'll need to install the Python Development Environment for Windows.

Open your web browser and navigate to the following website:

www.python.org/downloads/windows

Chapter 1: Getting Started

From the downloads page, select the 'executable installer' of latest stable release.

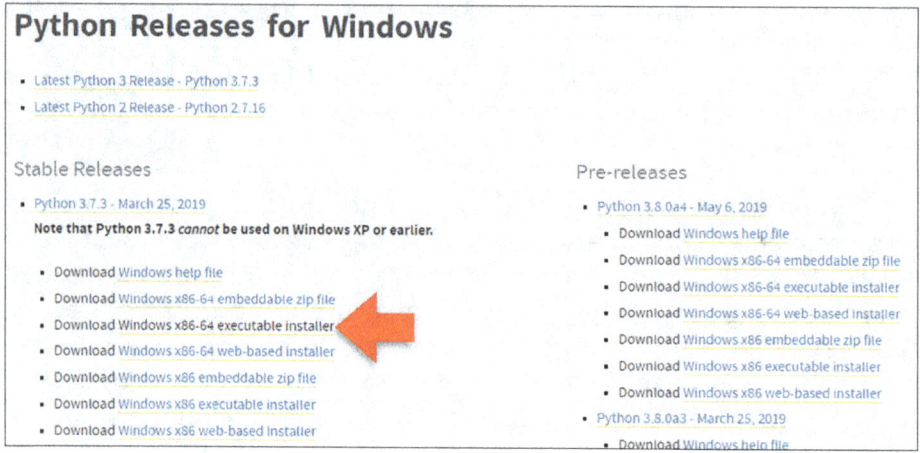

Click 'run' when prompted by your browser. Or click 'python-x.x.x-amd64.exe' if you're using Chrome.

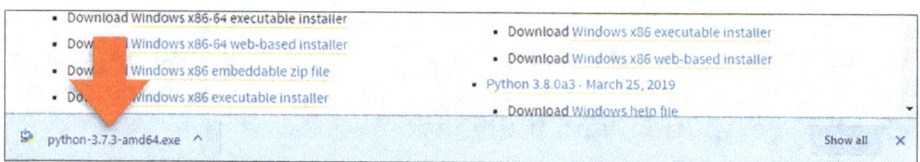

Once the installer starts, make sure 'add python 3.x to path' is selected, then click 'customize installation' to run through the steps to complete the installation.

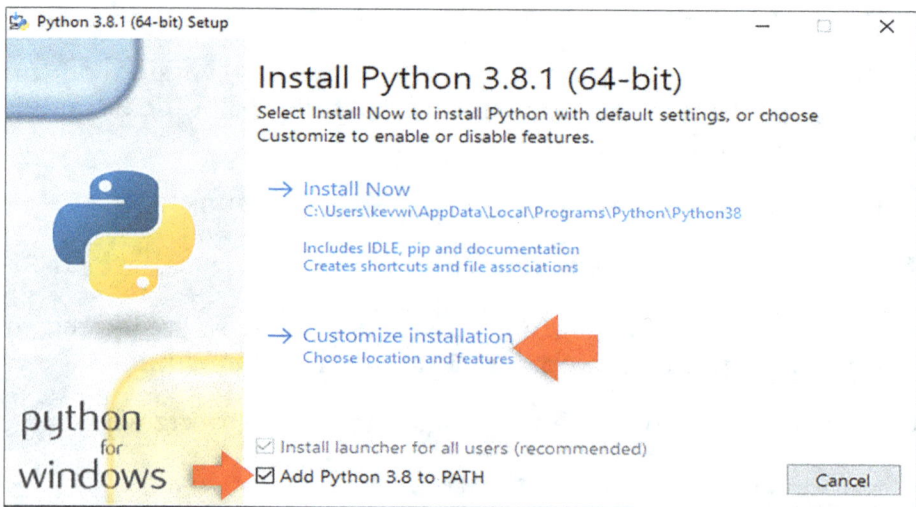

Chapter 1: Getting Started

Make sure you select all the tick boxes for all the optional features. Click 'next'.

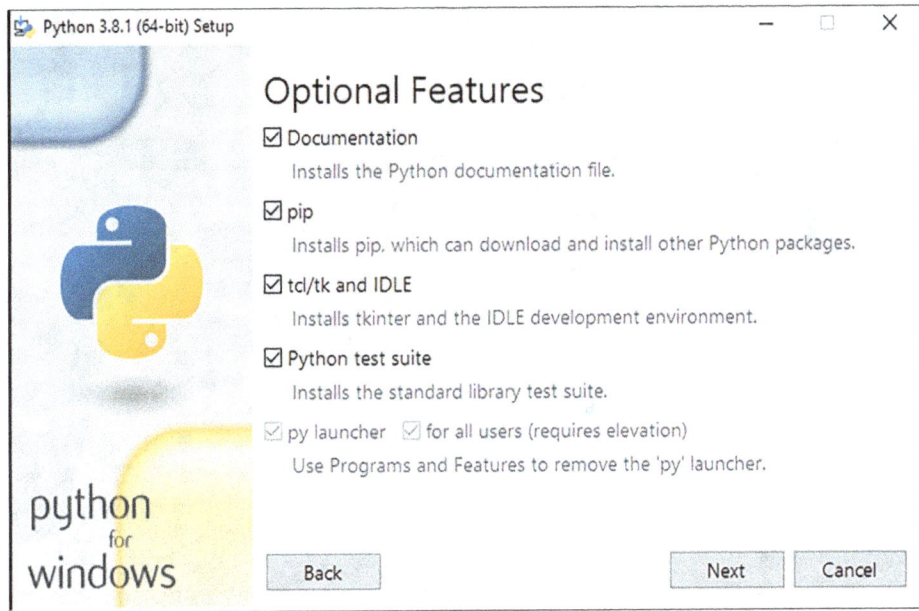

Make sure 'install for all users' is selected at the top of the dialog box. Click 'install' to begin.

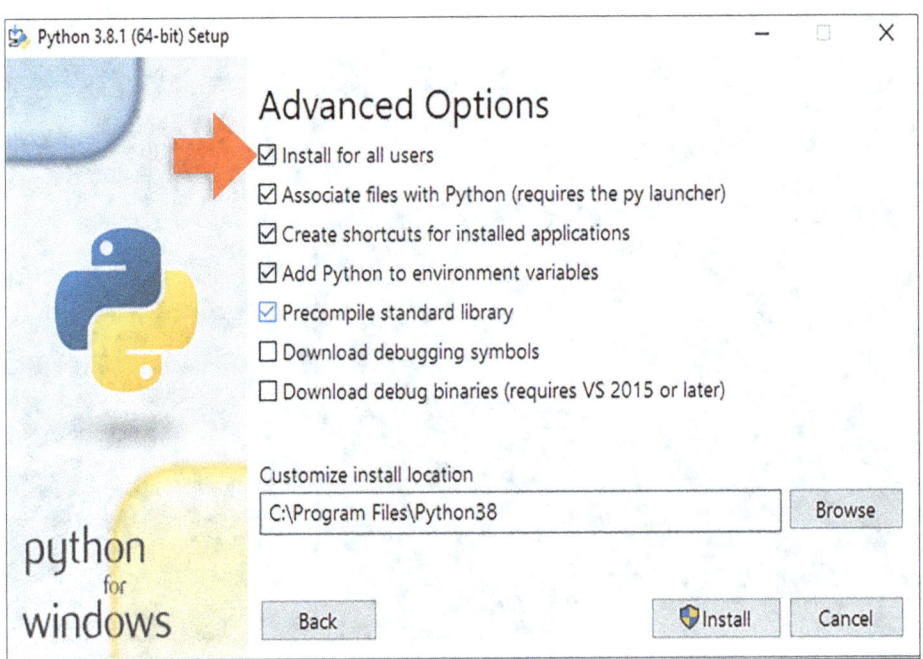

Chapter 1: Getting Started

Click 'disable path length limit' to make sure Python runs smoothly on Windows and allow long file names.

Click 'close' to finish the installation.

You'll find the Python Development Environment (IDLE) and the Python interpreter, in the Python folder on your start menu.

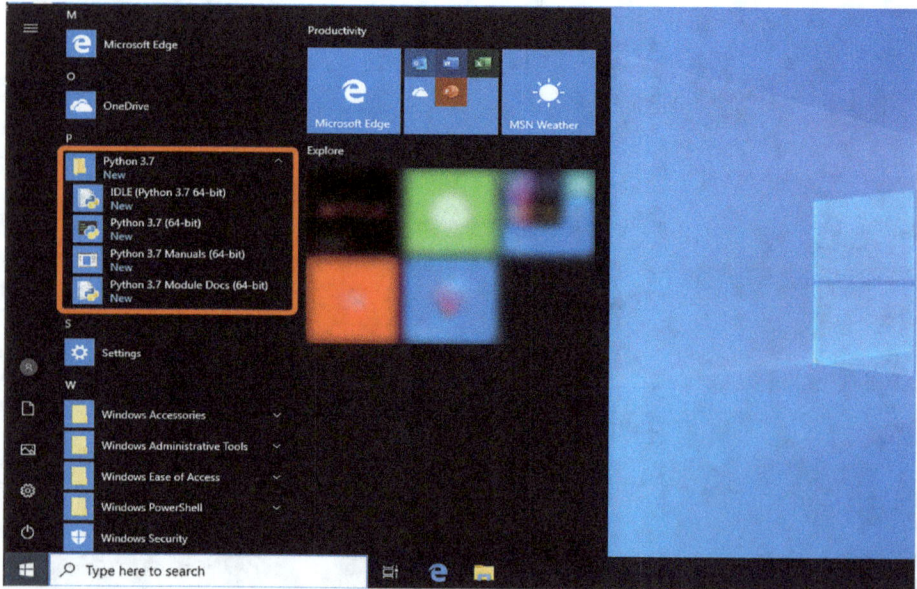

Chapter 1: Getting Started

Install on MacOS

To install Python 3 with the Official Installer, open your web browser and navigate to the following website

www.python.org/downloads/macos

Click download python.

You'll find the package in your downloads folder. Double click on the package to begin the installation

Run through the installation wizard. Click 'continue'.

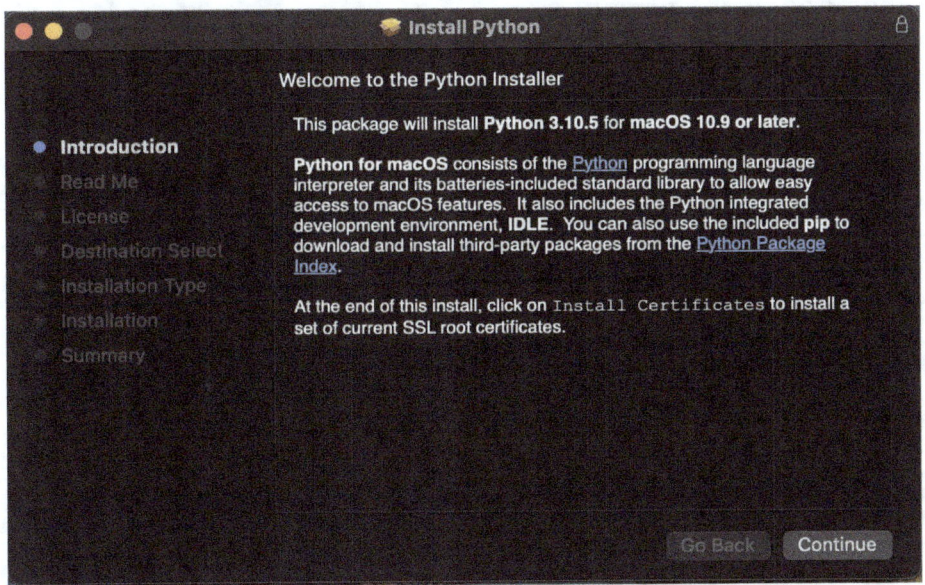

Once the installation is complete, you'll find python in the applications folder in finder, or on the launch pad.

Chapter 1: Getting Started

Install on Linux

If you are running a Linux distribution such as Ubuntu or have a Raspberry Pi, you can install python using the terminal. You'll find the terminal app in your applications. You can also press Control Alt T on your keyboard.

At the terminal command prompt, type the following commands. Press enter after each line.

`sudo apt update`

`sudo apt upgrade`

Type the following command to install Python.

`sudo apt install python3 -y`

Once the Python is installed, we need to install IDLE, the development environment. To do this, type the following command at the prompt

`sudo apt-get install idle3 -y`

Once installed, you'll find IDLE in your applications.

Or you can type the following command at the prompt

`idle3`

Chapter 1: Getting Started

Introduction to Pygame

Pygame is a library of Python modules designed for writing 2D video games. It provides tools and libraries to handle graphics, sound, input devices, timing, and game loops—all the building blocks needed to create interactive games.

While Python is not designed for high-performance game development, it excels as an educational language and a prototyping tool. Pygame builds on Python's simplicity to make real-time, interactive programming approachable.

It is especially well-suited for small 2D game development, where developers can build arcade-style games, platformers, puzzle games, and retro clones using built-in support for graphics, animation, and input.

Pygame is commonly used in educational tools and learning environments, where it helps learners grasp programming fundamentals, object-oriented design, and game logic through hands-on, visual projects.

It is also useful for rapid prototyping, allowing developers to quickly test gameplay mechanics, interaction designs, or visual ideas without the complexity or overhead of a full-scale game engine.

Chapter 1: Getting Started

Beyond games, Pygame can be used for multimedia applications such as interactive storybooks, audio visualizers, simple media players, and other programs that require real-time graphics and sound.

While Pygame is useful, it is not used in the games industry for developing commercial 3D games or complex, high-performance 2D titles due to its limitations in performance and scalability. Professional studios typically rely on feature-rich game engines that are designed for production environments.

Unity is used for mobile, indie, and mid-size commercial games and is based on the C# language.

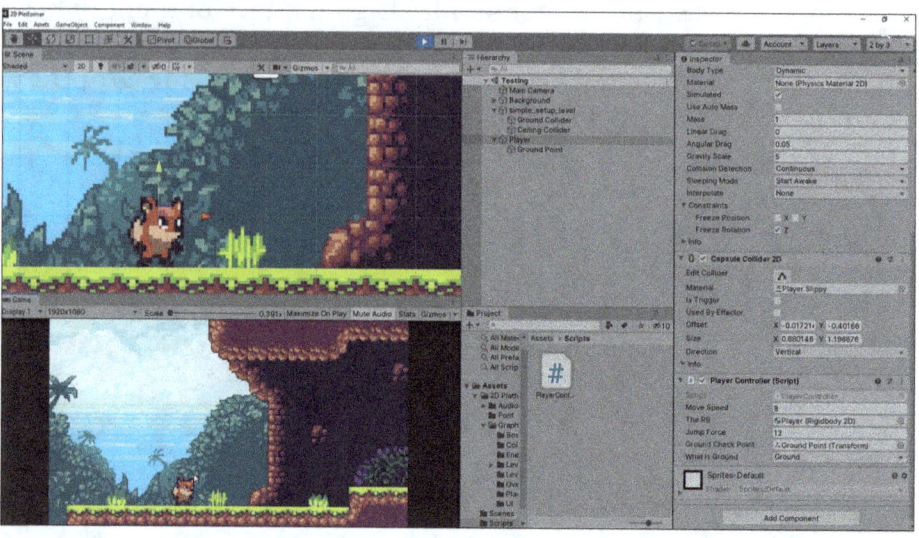

Unreal Engine is used for AAA, 3D, and high-performance titles, and supports both C++ and a visual scripting system called Blueprints.

Godot is a growing open-source engine used in smaller professional projects, and supports both GDScript and C#.

Large studios often build custom engines in C++ to meet specific technical and platform requirements, such as Rockstar's RAGE engine or Capcom's RE Engine.

Despite its limitations, Pygame remains a valuable tool for learning, experimentation, prototyping, and building simple games from scratch.

Chapter 1: Getting Started

Install Pygame

To install the module, open the command prompt, then type the following command.

```
pip install pygame
```

Once you press enter, the install will begin.

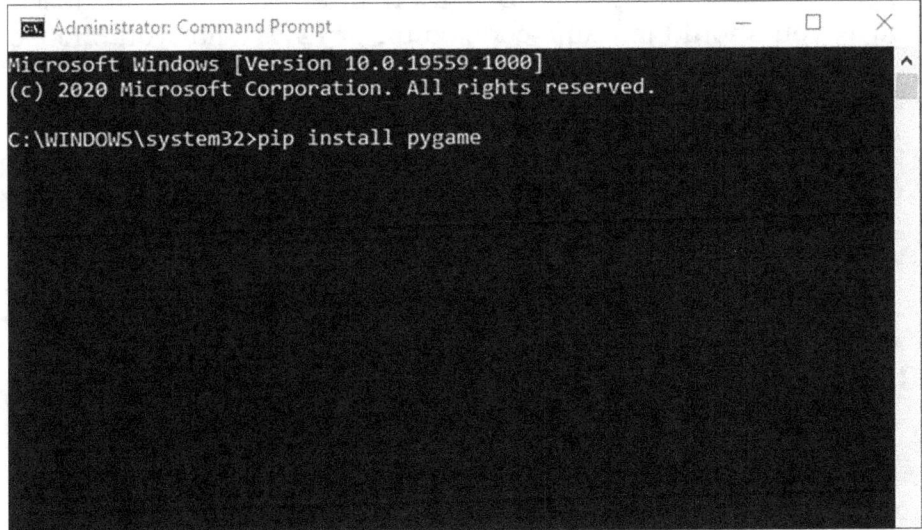

Allow the pip utility to download and install the module.

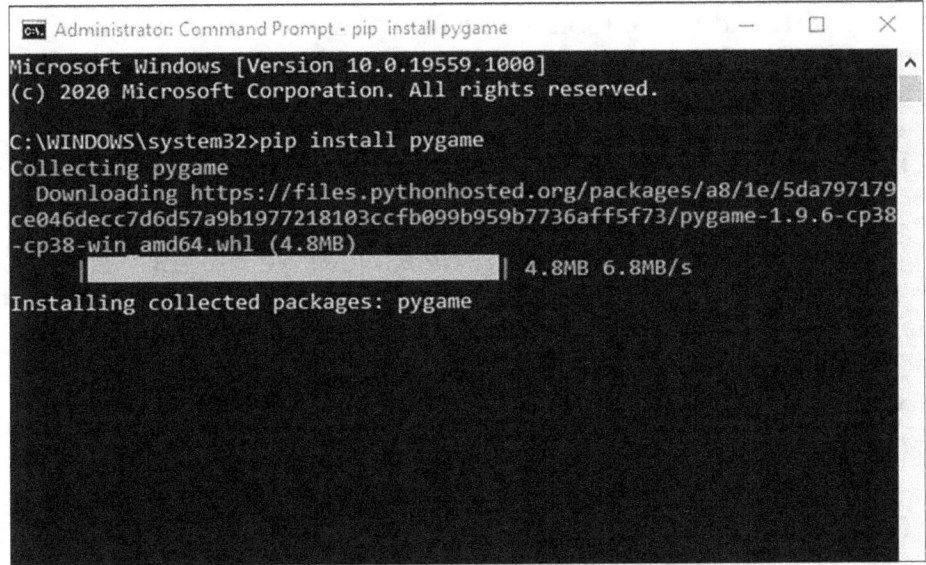

Chapter 1: Getting Started

Setting up your Development Environment

A good development environment enhances productivity by providing features such as code editing, debugging, and testing capabilities.

Once you have installed the python interpreter as discussed above, you should install a code editor or IDE. What you choose is personal preference and depends on the specific requirements of your project.

There are several code editors and Integrated Development Environments (IDEs) available for Python programming.

Try a few difference ones until you find the one that suits your needs the best.

Code Editor vs IDE

A code editor is a lightweight tool focused primarily on editing code. It provides features such as syntax highlighting, code completion, and basic code formatting. Some popular code editors are Visual Studio Code and Sublime Text.

An IDE is a comprehensive software suite that combines a code editor with additional tools and features specifically designed for software development. In addition to code editing capabilities, IDEs typically provide features like debugging, code refactoring, project management, and version control integration. Examples of popular IDEs include PyCharm, IDLE and Eclipse.

You should also consider an interactive computing environment. This is a software environment that allows you to interactively write and execute code while providing immediate feedback and results. Within this environment you can write code, run it, and see the output in real-time, facilitating an iterative and exploratory approach to programming.

Jupyter Notebook is a popular interactive computing environment that allows you to create and share documents containing live code, visualizations, and explanatory text.

Chapter 1: Getting Started

Visual Studio Code (VS Code)

Visual Studio Code is a lightweight and highly customizable code editor developed by Microsoft. It has excellent Python support with features such as IntelliSense which provides context-aware suggestions for functions, methods, variables, and modules as you type, helping you write code faster and with fewer errors. VS Code also offers debugging tools and a wide range of extensions that enhance Python development experience.

Go to the official website, download and install the software.

`code.visualstudio.com`

Next, install the Python Extension for VS Code. Click the Extensions icon on the left hand panel.

Search for "Python extension". Make sure it is the one published by Microsoft. Click Install.

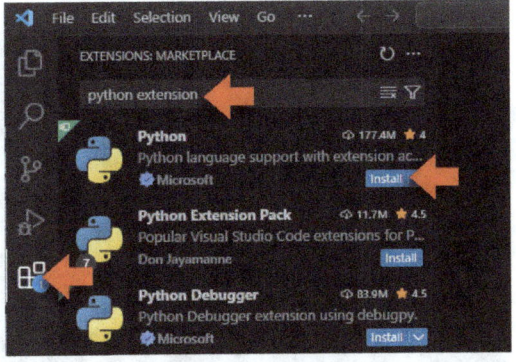

When you install the Python extension, it will automatically install the following components to provide the best Python development experience:

Pylance, a fast and feature-rich language server that powers IntelliSense, type checking, and code navigation using Pyright engine.

Python Debugger (debugpy), an in-editor tool that supports breakpoints, step-through execution, and variable inspection.

Chapter 1: Getting Started

Finally we need to create a folder where we can store all our programs. To do this, click the 'file' menu, then from the drop down, select 'open folder'.

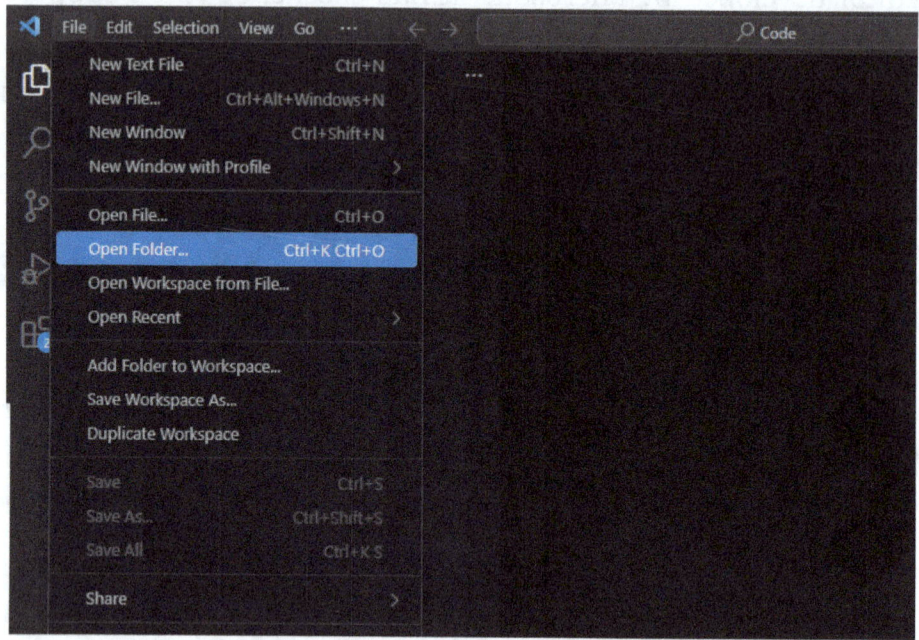

Navigate to your 'documents' folder, click on 'new folder', give your folder a meaningful name, then click 'select folder'.

This is the folder we'll use to store all our code.

Chapter 1: Getting Started

IDLE

IDLE (Integrated Development and Learning Environment) is a basic Python IDE that comes bundled with the Python installation. It provides a simple and beginner-friendly environment for writing, testing, and learning Python code — ideal for newcomers.

```python
import pygame

class GameWindow:
    def __init__(self, width, height):
        self.width = width
        self.height = height
        self.screen = pygame.display.set_mode((self.width, self.height))
        pygame.display.set_caption("My Game")

# Create an instance of the GameWindow class
game = GameWindow(800, 600)
```

```
Python 3.11.2 (tags/v3.11.2:878ead1, Feb  7 2023, 16:38:35) [MSC v.1934 64 bit (AMD64)] on win32
Type "help", "copyright", "credits" or "license()" for more information.
>>>
```

Chapter 1: Getting Started

While IDLE is a convenient option for beginners or when you need a lightweight and straightforward development environment, however it lacks some advanced features and customization options compared to other IDEs. As your Python programming skills and projects become more complex, you may want to explore other IDEs mentioned earlier to leverage additional functionalities and tools for efficient development.

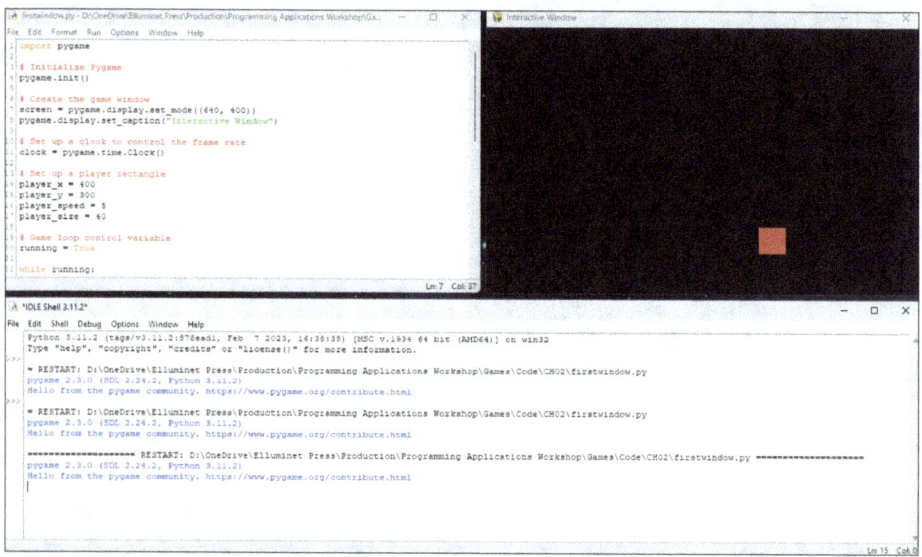

IDLE is a valuable tool for learning Python, exploring code interactively, and writing small programs. It is easy to launch, requires no setup, and provides immediate feedback, making it especially effective for teaching, experimentation, and introductory programming. However, as your skills progress and you begin working on more complex projects—such as games, multi-file applications, or programs that depend on third-party libraries—it is advisable to transition to a modern, extensible code editor such as Visual Studio Code. With its robust extension ecosystem, integrated debugger, terminal, and support for version control and virtual environments, Visual Studio Code offers a more powerful and flexible development environment that is better suited to professional programming workflows.

For this book, we will be using both IDLE and Visual Studio Code (VS Code). You are free to use either, depending on your preference and the complexity of the project.

Chapter 1: Getting Started

Organizing Your Projects

Before we begin writing any code, it's important to set up a clean, organized workspace on your computer. Game development projects typically involve multiple types of files — not just code, but also images, sound effects, music, level data, and saved game files. Keeping your files well structured from the start will save time, reduce bugs, and make your code easier to manage as your games grow in size and complexity.

Choose a convenient location on your system, such as the **Documents** folder, and create a new folder. For example:

```
python
```

Inside this folder, you'll create one subfolder per game project. For example:

```
python/
    └── my-invaders/
            ├── main.py
            ├── game.py
            └── images/
                    └── background.png
            └── sounds/
                    ├── bounce.wav
                    └── music.mp3
```

The **python** folder serves as the top-level workspace where all your Python projects are stored.

Inside it, you can create a folder for each of your projects. For example, the **my_invaders** folder contains all the files and resources needed for a game.

The **images** folder stores graphical assets used in the game, such as player sprites, enemies, and backgrounds.

The **sounds** folder holds all the audio assets for the game, including effects and music.

2

Intro to Python

Welcome to the world of Python programming — where you'll learn how to write code by creating your own games. Whether you've never written a single line of code or you're just getting started with Python, this chapter is your entry point into both programming and game development.

Instead of focusing on abstract examples like calculating tax or printing your name to the screen, we'll explore programming through the lens of video games. You'll learn how to move characters, respond to input, update scores, store game data, and control the logic that makes everything run — all using real Python code.

We've included all the source code for this chapter in the following repository:

elluminetpress.com/pyintro

Chapter 2: Introduction to Python

Statements

In Python, a statement is an instruction that the computer can execute. Every time you write a line of code that performs an action — like displaying a message, setting a variable, or updating a score — you are writing a statement.

Scan for Video

Think of a game like Pong. When the ball hits the paddle and bounces back, there's a statement in the code that tells it to reverse direction. When a player scores, another statement increases the score.

Let's start with a simple Python statement:

```
print("Welcome to the game!")
```

This statement tells Python to display text on the screen. In a real game, you might use print() to show messages for debugging or to track events during gameplay:

```
print("Player hit the wall")
print("Score increased by 10")
```

Python code is read and executed line by line, from top to bottom. Each line is usually a single statement. Here's a short sequence of statements that might represent the start of a game:

```
player_lives = 3
score = 0
print("Get ready!")
```

Each line here is a separate statement:

- One creates a variable for lives.
- Another sets the score.
- The last one prints a message.

These statements don't do much by themselves, but as you learn to combine them with conditions, loops, and input, they'll form the building blocks of a complete program or game.

29

Chapter 2: Introduction to Python

Reserved Words

Reserved words, also known as keywords, are words that have special meaning and are reserved for specific purposes. These words cannot be used as variable names or other identifiers because they are already used by the language itself.

Reserved Word	Meaning/Purpose
and	Logical operator for performing a logical AND operation
as	Used in context managers or aliasing
assert	Used to test if a given condition is true
break	Used to exit a loop prematurely
class	Used to define a class in object-oriented programming
continue	Used to skip the current iteration of a loop
def	Used to define a function
del	Used to delete a reference to an object
elif	Used with if statements to define additional conditions
else	Used with if statements or loops to define alternate behavior
except	Catches and handles exceptions
False	Boolean value representing false
finally	Used in exception handling to define code that always executes
for	Used to iterate over a sequence (e.g., list, string)
from	Used in import statements to specify the source module
global	Declares a global variable
if	Used to define a conditional statement
import	Used to import modules or specific attributes from modules
in	Used to test if a value is present in a sequence
is	Used for identity comparison
lambda	Used to create anonymous functions
None	Represents the absence of a value
nonlocal	Declares a variable from an outer (non-global) scope
not	Logical operator for performing a logical NOT operation
or	Logical operator for performing a logical OR operation
pass	Placeholder statement that does nothing
raise	Raises an exception
return	Used to return a value from a function
True	Boolean value representing true
try	Begins a block of code for exception handling
while	Used to create a loop that continues until a condition is met
with	Used to manage context for resources (e.g., file handling)
yield	Used in generator functions to produce a value

Indentation

Python uses indentation to define code blocks instead of using braces or keywords like "begin" and "end" as in other languages. Code blocks are usually indented using spaces or tabs (eg use four spaces per indentation level).

Consistent indentation is crucial in Python because it determines the grouping and hierarchy of code.

Chapter 2: Introduction to Python

It is important to note that mixing spaces and tabs for indentation can lead to errors, so it's best to choose one and stick to it.

In the example below, notice how the indentation is used to define the code blocks within the greet function. See page 43 for information on defining functions.

```
def greet(name):
    if len(name) > 0:
        print("Hello, " + name + "!")
    else:
        print("Hello there!")
    print("Nice to meet you.")

greet("Alice")
greet("Bob")
greet("")
```

The lines of code inside the if and else blocks are indented, indicating that they are part of those blocks. See page 39 for more information on if statements.

```
def greet(name):
    if len(name) > 0:
        print("Hello, " + name + "!")
    else:
        print("Hello there!")
    print("Nice to meet you.")
```

The line that prints "Nice to meet you" is indented at the same level as the if and else blocks, indicating that it is executed after the conditional statements.

See 'conditional statements' later in this chapter for more information on if-else statements.

Comments

When you're writing code, it's important to leave notes for yourself or other people who might read it later. That's where comments come in. A comment is a line of text in your code that Python ignores when the program runs.

Chapter 2: Introduction to Python

In a game, you might use comments to explain what part of the code controls the player, what triggers a win or loss, or why a certain value was chosen.

In Python, a comment begins with the # symbol:

```
# This sets the player's starting lives
player_lives = 3
```

Python ignores anything after the #, so this line only affects the human reading the code — not the computer.

Let's say you're setting up a simple shooting game. Your code might look like this:

```
# Player starts with 3 lives
player_lives = 3

# Score starts at 0
score = 0

# Display welcome message
print("Welcome to Space Blaster!")
```

For longer explanations, you'll sometimes see triple quotes. These create a multi-line string literal.

```
'''
This is a multi-line string
that takes up more than one line.
'''
```

In Python, only lines starting with # are real comments. When a triple-quoted string appears as the first line inside a file, class, or function, it becomes a docstring. If it is not used as a docstring or assigned to a variable, the string is created and then immediately discarded, so it does not affect how the program runs. These strings do not change what the code does, but can be used to provide longer documentation for files, classes, or functions, which becomes useful as your game grows in complexity.

- Use comments to explain why the code does something
- To explain sections of code (e.g., setup, main loop, scoring)
- To disable a line temporarily while testing

Chapter 2: Introduction to Python

Variables

A variable is a way to store a value that your program can use and change later. Think of variables as labeled boxes that hold things like the player's score, position, speed, or number of lives.

In a game, you use variables for almost everything: the health of a character, the speed of a bullet, the level the player is on — all of these are stored in variables so they can change as the game runs.

To create a variable, you choose a name and use the = sign (the assignment operator) to assign a value:

Scan for Video

```
score = 0
player_lives = 3
level = 1
```

Now your program remembers:

- The score starts at 0
- The player has 3 lives
- You're on level 1

You can later update these variables as the game progresses:

```
score = score + 10              # Add 10 to score
player_lives = player_lives - 1 # Lose a life
level = level + 1               # Go to next level
```

You can name your variables almost anything, but they:

- Must start with a letter or underscore
- Can contain letters, numbers, and underscores
- Can't be the same as any Python reserved words
- Should be descriptive

33

Chapter 2: Introduction to Python

Arrays, Lists and Tuples

An array is a mutable, ordered sequence of elements restricted to a single data type, provided by Python's array module, but it is rarely used. A list is a mutable, ordered sequence that can hold mixed data types. Mutable means the elements can be changed after creation. Ordered means the elements can be indexed. Think of a list as a row of numbered boxes, each holding one element. For example: alien, robot, slime, ship, or rocket, as we can see in the diagram below.

Scan for Video

In Python, a list is written using square brackets [ ]:

```
high_scores = [1000, 800, 600, 400, 200]
```

Here above, the high_scores list holds five score values — from highest to lowest. You can also make a list of strings:

```
enemy_types = ["alien", "robot", "slime"]
```

Or a list of positions:

```
enemy_positions = [100, 150, 300, 400]
```

Each element in a list has an index, starting from 0:

```
print(high_scores[0])    # prints 1000
print(enemy_types[1])    # prints "robot"
```

If you want to get the last item:

```
print(high_scores[-1])   # prints 200
```

If you want to change the List elements, you can update values in a list using the index:

```
high_scores[0] = 1200
enemy_types[2] = "boss"
```

You can add new elements to the end of the list with append():

```
enemy_positions.append(500)
```

Chapter 2: Introduction to Python

And remove elements with remove() or pop():

```
enemy_types.remove("robot")   # removes value 'robot'
enemy_positions.pop(0)        # removes the first item
```

Lists are useful for storing enemy positions, levels and maps, collected items, active bullets, and power-up timers.

Tuples look similar to lists, but they are written with parentheses () instead of square brackets, and they cannot be changed once created — although they can contain mutable objects such as lists or dictionaries. This makes them useful for fixed data such as coordinates, colors, or sizes.

```
player_start = (50, 300)     # x, y position
enemy_color = (255, 0, 0)    # RGB red
```

Dictionaries

Scan for Video

A dictionary is a way to store values using key-value pairs. Think of it as a box with labels on it. Instead of remembering values by position like a list, you give each item a name (the key) so you can retrieve it directly. In game development, dictionaries are useful for storing related data about a player, enemy, or object — such as their name, score, health, or position.

Here's an example of a dictionary that stores information about a player:

```
player = {
    "name": "Hero",
    "health": 100,
    "lives": 3,
    "score": 0
}
```

Each entry is made up of a key (like "name", "health"), and a value (like "Hero", 100).

To get a value, use the key inside square brackets:

```
print(player["name"])      # prints "Hero"
print(player["score"])     # prints 0
```

35

Chapter 2: Introduction to Python

You can also use .get() to safely retrieve values:

```
print(player.get("lives"))   # prints 3
```

To change a value, assign a new value to the key:

```
player["score"] = 50
player["health"] -= 10
```

You can add new data to the dictionary:

```
player["level"] = 1
```

Now the player dictionary includes a "level" key with value 1.

To remove a key-value pair, use del:

```
del player["lives"]
```

Dictionaries are perfect for grouping together properties of a game object. For example, you might use one to represent an enemy:

```
enemy = {
    "type": "robot",
    "x": 150,
    "y": 300,
    "speed": 4
}
```

This keeps related data neatly organized and easy to manage — especially when combined with loops or functions.

Operators

Operators are special symbols that perform operations on values or variables.

You use them to do things like add scores, compare lives, or update positions.

Operators are essential for controlling game logic — whether you're checking collisions, adding points, or moving characters across the screen.

Scan for Video

Chapter 2: Introduction to Python

Arithmetic Operators

Arithmetic operators are used with numeric data types such as integers and floats.

Operator	Purpose	Example	Result
+	Addition	`score + 10`	Adds 10 to score
-	Subtraction	`lives - 1`	Subtracts a life
*	Multiplication	`speed * 2`	Multiplies speed by 2
/	Division	`distance / 2`	Divides distance by 2
//	Floor division	`7 // 2`	Results in 3
%	Modulo	`level % 2`	Remainder (used for even/odd checks)
**	Exponentiation	`2 ** 3`	8 (2 to the power of 3)

In a game, you might use arithmetic to increase a score or move a player:

```
score = score + 100
player_x = player_x + speed
```

Comparison Operators

These compare two values and return True or False — essential for game decisions.

Operator	Meaning	Example
==	Equal to	`lives == 0`
!=	Not equal to	`score != 1000`
>	Greater than	`score > high_score`
<	Less than	`lives < max_lives`
>=	Greater or equal	`level >= 10`
<=	Less or equal	`speed <= 5`

For example:

```
if player_lives == 0:
    print("Game Over")
```

Chapter 2: Introduction to Python

Logical Operators

These let you combine multiple conditions — great for complex rules in games:

Operator	Description	Example
and	Both conditions must be true	`if score > 100 and level == 2:`
or	Either condition can be true	`if key == "a" or key == "left":`
not	Reverses the result	`if not game_running:`

Assignment Operators

Assignment operators are used to assign values to variables. They also allow you to modify the value of a variable by performing an operation and assigning the result back to the variable.

Operator	Description
Assignment (=)	Assigns a value to a variable.
Addition assignment (+=)	Adds a value to the variable and assigns the result.
Subtraction assignment (-=)	Subtracts a value from the variable and assigns the result.
Multiplication assignment (*=)	Multiplies the variable by a value and assigns the result.
Division assignment (/=)	Divides the variable by a value and assigns the result.
Modulo assignment (%=)	Performs modulo operation on the variable and assigns the result.

These are shorthand ways to update a variable's value, and are very common in game loops where things change continuously

```
score += 10    # Same as: score = score + 10
lives -= 1     # Same as: lives = lives - 1
```

They allow you to simplify complex expressions, reduce repetition, and make your game logic easier to follow.

So instead of writing `score = score + 10` to increment the player's score, we can write `score += 10`

Chapter 2: Introduction to Python

Conditional Statements

In programming, conditional statements allow you to make decisions. You use them to check if something is true — and then run a specific block of code based on the result. This is how your game knows when to respond to a key press, trigger a game over, or unlock the next level.

The if Statement

The most basic conditional is the if statement:

```
if player_lives == 0:
    print("Game Over")
```

This checks whether player_lives is equal to 0. If it is, the message is displayed.

Using if...else

You can add an else clause to handle what happens when the condition is not true:

```
if score >= 1000:
    print("You win!")
else:
    print("Keep going!")
```

Adding More Conditions with elif

When you need to check multiple different conditions, use elif (short for "else if"):

```
if score >= 1000:
    print("You win!")
elif score >= 500:
    print("Halfway there!")
else:
    print("Keep trying!")
```

The game checks each condition in order and runs the first one that's true.

39

Chapter 2: Introduction to Python

Indentation Matters

In Python, the code under an if, elif, or else must be indented. This tells Python which lines belong to the condition.

```
if player_lives == 0:
    print("Game Over")
    running = False
```

If you don't indent properly, Python will give you an error.

Match Statements

The match statement is a newer feature in Python (introduced in Python 3.10) that provides a clean and readable way to compare a value against several possible options. It's similar to a switch statement in other languages like C or JavaScript.

In games, match can be useful for handling input commands, game states, or object types — wherever you need to run different code based on a single value. Here's how a match statement works:

```
match command:
    case "start":
        print("Game started")
    case "pause":
        print("Game paused")
    case "quit":
        print("Exiting game")
```

Python checks the value of command and runs the matching case block. If command = "pause", the output will be:

```
Game paused
```

Imagine you have different enemy types and want to perform actions based on their type:

```
enemy_type = "slime"
match enemy_type:
    case "slime":
        print("Slime jumps")
```

Chapter 2: Introduction to Python

```
    case "robot":
        print("Robot shoots lasers")
    case "alien":
        print("Alien teleports")
```

You can also combine conditions or use wildcards:

```
match player_lives:
    case 3:
        print("Full health")
    case 2 | 1:
        print("Low health")
    case 0:
        print("Game Over")
```

Each case is checked from top to bottom. If no case matches, nothing happens (unless you use a wildcard _).

```
match direction:
    case "left":
        move_left()
    case "right":
        move_right()
    case _:
        print("Invalid direction")
```

Why Use match? It's cleaner and easier to read than multiple if... elif statements. It's useful when comparing one value to multiple possible cases and works well for game commands, game states, or action handlers.

Loops

In games, certain actions happen repeatedly — like redrawing the screen, checking for input, moving characters, or updating timers. To make this possible, you use loops. A loop lets you repeat a block of code multiple times — or even forever. Without loops, your game would only run one frame and immediately quit.

Python has two main types of loops, the while loop and the for loop.

Chapter 2: Introduction to Python

While Loops

While Loops keep the Game Running. The while loop runs as long as a condition is true. Here's a basic game loop:

```
running = True
while running:
    for event in pygame.event.get():
        if event.type == pygame.QUIT:
            running = False
```

This loop keeps the game running until the player closes the window. Inside the loop, you can handle input, move objects, check collisions, and draw to the screen — again and again, every frame.

For Loops

The for loop is useful when you want to repeat something a specific number of times — like spawning enemies or looping through a list of scores.

```
for i in range(5):
    print("Spawning enemy", i)
```

This loop runs 5 times and prints:

```
Spawning enemy 0
Spawning enemy 1
Spawning enemy 2
Spawning enemy 3
Spawning enemy 4
```

You can also use for to loop through a list:

```
enemies = ["slime", "robot", "alien"]
for enemy in enemies:
    print(enemy, "appears!")
```

For loops are a core part of many game mechanics, making it easy to repeat actions, process lists of items, or cycle through levels, animations, or game events.

Chapter 2: Introduction to Python

Breaking Out of a Loop

You can stop a loop early using the break statement:

```
for bullet in bullets:
    if bullet.hit_enemy():
        print("Hit!")
        break
```

Skipping a Turn in the Loop

Use continue to skip the rest of the current loop and move to the next one:

```
for score in high_scores:
    if score == 0:
        continue  # skip zero scores
    print("Score:", score)
```

Loops in Game Development

Loops are everywhere in games. The main game loop that keeps the game running is a while loop. Iterating through enemies, bullets, or levels typically uses for loops. Repeating animations or effects, and checking or updating the game state every frame, also rely on loop structures. Learning how loops work is key to writing real-time games that respond smoothly and consistently.

Functions

Functions are blocks of code that perform a specific task. In games, functions help you organize your code into reusable actions like moving a character, checking for collisions, drawing the screen, or playing sounds.

Think of a function like a mini-program that you can call whenever you need it. Functions make your code easier to read, easier to reuse, and easier to debug.

You define a function using the def keyword:

43

Chapter 2: Introduction to Python

```
def greet_player():
    print("Welcome to the game!")
```

This function doesn't take any inputs, but it prints a greeting. To use (or call) it:

```
greet_player()
```

Functions with Parameters

You can make a function more flexible by giving it parameters — placeholders for input values the function can work with:

```
def add_score(current_score, points):
    return current_score + points
```

In this example, **current_score** and **points** are parameters. They define what kind of data the function expects when it's called. You call the function by passing arguments — the actual values you want the function to use:

```
score = add_score(score, 100)
```

Here, **score** and **100** are arguments. They are passed into the function, assigned to the corresponding parameters, and used to calculate the new score.

Functions are essential to building games that are modular, maintainable, and easy to scale. You'll use them in every game project — from drawing sprites to handling input to spawning enemies.

Returning Values from Functions

Most often you'll want a function not just to do something, but to give something back — like a score calculation, a player's speed, or a newly generated enemy position.

To do this, functions use the return keyword. When a function returns a value, it sends that value back to wherever the function was called. You can then store the result in a variable or use it immediately in another calculation.

Chapter 2: Introduction to Python

The function below calculates the player's speed based on the current level. As the level increases, so does the speed.

```
def get_player_speed(level):
    return 5 + level
```

You can call it like this:

```
speed = get_player_speed(3)   # speed is now 8
```

The function returns the result of 5 + **level** (the value passed into the function (3 in this case)), and that value is stored in the variable **speed**.

This approach makes your functions reusable and adaptable — perfect for tasks you'll repeat throughout your games, like updating scores, calculating damage, or positioning sprites.

Classes & Objects

In game programming, classes are incredibly useful. You can create classes for things like players, enemies, bullets, levels, or anything else that needs its own data and logic.

Scan for Video

A class is a blueprint for creating objects. It defines the attributes (data) and methods (behaviors) that the objects of that class will use. Classes are defined using the class keyword.

Attributes are variables that hold data associated with an object. They are defined within the class and can be accessed and modified using dot notation: **object.attribute**

Methods are functions defined within a class that perform specific actions or operations on the object's data. They are associated with the class and can be called using dot notation **object.method()**

This approach is known as object oriented programming.

Defining a Class & Adding Attributes

In Python, classes are used to model real-world entities and game components—such as players, enemies, projectiles, or game levels—by encapsulating related data and functionality into a single logical unit.

45

Chapter 2: Introduction to Python

You define a class using the class keyword followed by the name of the class. Note classes usually start with a capital letter.

```
class Player:
    def __init__(self, name, health):
        self.name = name
        self.health = health
```

class Player: defines a new class called Player

__init__ (two underscores before and after), is a special method called a constructor. It runs when a new object is created. This method initializes the new object with default or user-provided values known as attributes. Think of it as the setup function for a new instance—it gives the object its initial state.

self refers to the current instance of the class — the specific object being created.

self.name and **self.health** are instance variables — they store information for that object.

Adding Methods

Methods are functions defined within a class that perform specific actions or operations using the object's data—its attributes. Methods are used to define the behavior of an object.

In Python, you define a method just like a regular function, but it must be placed inside the class definition and include self as the first parameter. Here **self** refers to the instance of the class that is calling the method. This allows the method to access and modify the object's attributes and call other methods defined in the same class. Without **self**, the method would have no way of knowing which specific object it is operating on.

You can define methods as follows.

```
class Player:
    def __init__(self, name, health):
    self.name = name
    self.health = health

    def take_damage(self, amount):
        self.health -= amount
        print(self.name, "takes", amount, "damage!")
```

Chapter 2: Introduction to Python

Creating Objects

Once a class has been defined, you can use it to create actual objects, also called instances. An object is a specific version of the class with its own unique data stored in attributes.

To create a player object from the Player class:

```
player1 = Player("Hero", 100)
print(player1.name)            # Hero
print(player1.health)          # 100
```

Why Use Classes in Games?

Let's say you have multiple enemies in your game. Instead of creating separate variables for each one:

```
enemy1_x = 100
enemy1_y = 200
enemy2_x = 150
enemy2_y = 250
```

You can define an Enemy class and make each enemy its own object:

```
class Enemy:
    def __init__(self, x, y):
        self.x = x
        self.y = y
        self.health = 100
```

Now you can create enemy objects like this:

```
enemy1 = Enemy(100, 200)
enemy2 = Enemy(150, 250)
```

Each enemy has its own position and health, but they all follow the same blueprint.

Using classes keeps your code organized and scalable. Instead of repeating the same logic for each enemy, you can write it once in the class and reuse it across all instances. This makes it easier to manage behaviors like movement, attacking, or taking damage.

Chapter 2: Introduction to Python

File Handling

Games often need to save and load information — such as high scores, level data, player progress, or settings. In Python, you can store and retrieve data using files. This process is called file handling.

Python makes it easy to work with files using the built-in **open()** function, along with methods like **.read()**, **.write()**, and **.close()**.

In the parenthesis, list the filename followed by the mode.

```
with open("filename", "mode") as file:
```

The **filename** is a string that specifies the name (and optionally the path) of the file we want to open (e.g., "scores.txt"). If it's in a different folder, provide the path (e.g., "data/scores.txt" or "C:\\Games\data\scores.txt").

The **mode** specifies how a file should be opened and accessed. Let's take a look at the common modes:

- **"r"** stands for read mode (default) and opens a file for reading only. The file needs to exist.

- **"w"** stands for write mode and opens a file for writing. This mode will create a new file if it doesn't exist or truncates the file if it exists.

- **"a"** stands for append mode and opens the file for appending. Data will be written at the end of the file.

- **"r+"** stands for read and write mode. Opens the file for both reading and writing. The file must exist.

- **"w+"** stands for write and read mode. Similar to "r+", but it truncates the file to zero length if it exists or creates a new file if it doesn't exist.

- **"a+"** stands for append and read mode. Opens the file for both appending and reading. Data written to the file is added at the end, and the file is not truncated. It creates a new file if it doesn't exist.

Chapter 2: Introduction to Python

Writing to a File

This example writes a new high score to a text file:

```
with open("scores.txt", "w") as file:
    file.write("2500")
```

"scores.txt" is the name of the file to write to (it will be created if it doesn't exist).

"w" means write mode — it will overwrite any existing content.

file.write() sends the text "2500" into the file.

with ... as file: automatically closes the file when done.

You can use this to save scores, settings, or even level data in your games.

Reading from a File

Later, you might want to read that score back in:

```
with open("scores.txt", "r") as file:
    high_score = file.read()
print("High Score:", high_score)
```

"scores.txt" is the name of the file to read from.

"r" means read mode.

.read() returns the entire content of the file as a string.

Appending to a File

If you want to add new data to the end of a file without deleting the old content, use "a" (append mode):

```
with open("scores.txt", "a") as file:
    file.write("Player1: 1800\n")
```

"scores.txt" is the name of the file to append to.

"a" means append mode.

file.write() appends the text "1800" into the end of file.

49

Chapter 2: Introduction to Python

This is useful if you're saving multiple scores, logs, or event histories.

Real-World Game Example

Imagine a simple function to check and update the high score:

```
def update_high_score(score):
    with open("scores.txt", "r") as file:
        current_high = int(file.read())
    if score > current_high:
        with open("scores.txt", "w") as file:
            file.write(str(score))
```

This checks the stored score, compares it to the current one, and updates the file if you beat the record.

Using Modules

In Python, a module is a file containing Python code — usually functions, classes, or variables — that you can import and use in other scripts. Modules help you organize your code and reuse functionality across different parts of your game.

Scan for Video

Think of a module like a toolkit. Instead of writing everything in one file, you can split your game into separate files — one for player logic, one for enemies, one for the game engine — and then bring them together using imports.

Using Third Party Modules

Python comes with many built-in and third party modules. You've already used some, like:

pygame is a library for building games and multimedia applications, providing functionality for graphics rendering, sound playback, and user input handling.

tkinter is the standard Python interface to the Tk GUI toolkit. It provides a set of tools for building graphical user interfaces, including various widgets (buttons, labels, entry fields, etc.) that

Chapter 2: Introduction to Python

you can use to create windows, dialogs, and other GUI elements.

random is used to generate random numbers. Ideal for creating unpredictable gameplay elements such as enemy positions, power-up drops, or chance-based events.

time provides time-related functions. Useful for adding delays, controlling timing, and measuring performance.

math gives access to mathematical functions like square roots, trigonometry, rounding, and more — essential for movement, physics, or calculating angles.

os lets you interact with the operating system. You can check if a file exists, create folders, or handle file paths in a way that works on different platforms.

Importing Libraries

To use any of these libraries in your programs, you'll need to import them. To do this use the import keyword followed by the library name. For example

```
import pygame
```

To call a function from an imported module or library use

```
pygame.function_name()
```

For example:

Create a game window

```
pygame.display.set_mode((800, 600))
```

Control the game's frame rate

```
pygame.time.Clock()
```

Load a sound effect

```
pygame.mixer.Sound("explosion.wav")
```

Each function belongs to a part of the pygame module — such as display, time, or mixer — and is accessed using dot notation.

Chapter 2: Introduction to Python

This structure keeps your code organized and makes it easy to use powerful features provided by external libraries like Pygame.

Creating your Own

As your programs grow larger, you'll want to split your code into multiple files to keep things organized. Python makes this easy by letting you create your own modules.

Scan for Video

A module is simply a Python file that contains functions, variables, or classes. You can then import that file into another Python program, just like you import built-in libraries.

Suppose you create a file called player.py:

```
# player.py
class Player:
    def __init__(self, x, y):
        self.x = x
        self.y = y
        self.health = 100

    def move(self, dx, dy):
        self.x += dx
        self.y += dy
```

Now in your main game file (main.py), you can import and use that class:

```
import player

p1 = player.Player(100, 200)
```

Exercises

1. What is a Python statement? Give three examples of statements that might appear in a simple game.

2. Why is indentation important in Python? What will happen if you don't indent your code correctly inside an if statement or loop?

Chapter 2: Introduction to Python

3. What is a comment in Python? How do you write a single-line and a multi-line comment?

4. What's the difference between a list and a dictionary? Give an example of how each could be used in a game.

5. Explain what a function is and why functions are useful.

6. What does the match statement do in Python, and how is it different from using if and elif?

7. What is the difference between a while loop and a for loop? When would you use each?

8. In object-oriented programming, what is a class? How is it used to model game objects like players or enemies?

9. What are the main file modes in Python? What does each one do?

10. How do you import a Python module, and why would you create your own?

Challenge

Create a simple program that uses a class to model a player in a game. The class should store the player's name, score, and number of lives. It should also include methods to take damage, increase score, and check if the game is over.

Your program should:
- Define a Player class with the following:
- __init__() method to set up name, score (default 0), and lives (default 3)
- add_score(points) method to increase the score
- take_damage() method to decrease lives by 1
- is_game_over() method to return True if lives == 0
- Create a player object called player1 with the name "Hero"
    - Add random amounts of score (e.g. 100, 200, etc.)
    - Reduce lives each turn
    - Printing the player's status after each turn
    - At the end, print "Game Over" if lives reach 0
- Save the final score to a file named final_score.txt

3

Game Windows & Loops

In this chapter, we'll take the first practical step toward building real games with Python and Pygame — by creating a game window. This window is the canvas where everything in the game will be drawn, updated, and displayed. It's the foundation for all interaction, animation, and visual effects.

You'll learn how to write a basic Pygame program that opens a window, responds to user input, and stays active using a game loop.

We've included all the source code for this chapter in the following repository:

elluminetpress.com/gameloops

Chapter 3: Game Windows & Loops

Creating a Game Window

Scan for Video

The first thing we need to do is create a game window. The game window is the visible area of the screen where the game is displayed — it's the frame or canvas where all the action happens.

Before writing any code, it's important to organise your work properly. First, create a new folder to store your files. It's good practice to keep each game or project in its own folder, so everything stays organised and easy to manage. In VS Code explorer click 'new folder' icon. Give the folder a meaningful name (e.g., CH03).

Create a new file, e.g., main.py

To create a window for a game, first import the Pygame library and initialise it.

```
import pygame
pygame.init()
```

Next, we define the width and height of the game window in pixels. You can change these values later depending on your game's needs.

```
width = 800
height = 600
```

We use this to create the actual game window — a space where all graphics will be drawn. This returns a display Surface object stored in the screen variable.

```
screen = pygame.display.set_mode((width, height))
```

55

Chapter 3: Game Windows & Loops

You can add a caption to the window's title bar. Enter a meaningful name to identify your game.

`pygame.display.set_caption("My Game")`

We create a Boolean variable that keeps track of whether the game is running. When running is True, the game loop continues.

`running = True`

Next, we add the game loop. This keeps the window open and ready to update the screen, process events, and respond to input — repeating many times per second.

`while running:`

Inside the main game loop, we add the event loop. This checks for and responds to all the user and system-generated events. These events may include mouse clicks, keyboard input, game controller actions, or system-level requests, such as the player attempting to close the window. We'll look at this in more detail later in chapter 5.

```
for event in pygame.event.get():
    if event.type == pygame.QUIT:
        running = False
```

After the loop ends, this shuts down all Pygame modules and closes the window properly.

`pygame.quit()`

To run the program, click the 'play' icon on the top right of the screen.

```
main.py
CH02 > main.py > ...
 1    import pygame
 2
 3    # Initialize Pygame
 4    pygame.init()
 5
 6    # Set up the display
 7    width = 800
 8    height = 600
 9    screen = pygame.display.set_mode((width, height))
10    pygame.display.set_caption("My Game")
11
12    # Game loop
13    running = True
14    while running:
15        for event in pygame.event.get():
16            if event.type == pygame.QUIT:
17                running = False
18
19    # Quit Pygame
20    pygame.quit()
```

Chapter 3: Game Windows & Loops

We should end up with a blank window.

Once we have this set up, we can start building games. We can add the following.

- The background (could be a color or image)
- Sprites and characters
- Score and status bars
- Animations and effects
- User interface elements (buttons, menus, HUDs)

What Is a Game Loop?

A game loop is the fundamental structure that drives nearly every real-time game. Unlike standard programs that run line by line and then exit, games must stay open, responsive, and constantly updating. To achieve this, the game enters a loop that repeats continuously while the game is running.

Each time the loop executes, it performs three main tasks:

1. Handle user input (keyboard, mouse, controller)
2. Update the game state (player movement, collisions, scores)
3. Draw the updated state to the screen

This loop runs many times per second to create a smooth, real-time experience. For example 60 frames per second (FPS).

Chapter 3: Game Windows & Loops

The code template below provides the foundational structure for building 2D games in Python using the Pygame library. It defines the essential components of a game loop, including event handling, game state updates, rendering, and frame rate control. Use this as a starting point for any Pygame project, just insert your own logic, drawing routines, and game mechanics where indicated.

```python
# Import & Initialize Pygame
import pygame
pygame.init()

# Set up display
WIDTH = 800
HEIGHT = 600
screen = pygame.display.set_mode((WIDTH, HEIGHT))
pygame.display.set_caption("My Game")

# Set up clock for frame rate control
clock = pygame.time.Clock()
FPS = 60                    # Target frames per second

# Game state variables
running = True

# --- Main Game Loop ---
while running:
    # 1 --- Handle Input: mouse, keyboard, controller---
    for event in pygame.event.get():
        if event.type == pygame.QUIT:
            running = False

    # 2 --- Update Game State ---
    # Add your game logic here

    # 3 --- Draw Frame ---
    screen.fill((0, 0, 0))       # Clear screen

    # Draw game elements here

    pygame.display.flip()        # Update display

    # 4 --- Limit Frame Rate ---
    clock.tick(FPS)

# Clean exit
pygame.quit()
```

Chapter 3: Game Windows & Loops

The template begins by importing and initializing Pygame using **pygame.init()** which activates all the internal systems required for graphics, sound, and input handling. This initialization step is normally performed at the start of a Pygame program to initialise all available Pygame modules.

Next, the display window is configured using **pygame.display.set_mode()** which creates a display surface with the given dimensions (800 by 600 pixels in this case). This screen surface is where all game elements will be drawn. A title for the window is set using **pygame.display.set_caption()** which helps identify the game when it's running.

We then create a Clock object from **pygame.time** which is used to control how fast the game loop runs.

A variable named **running** is initialized to True. This acts as a flag to control whether the game loop should continue executing. When the player closes the window, the flag is set to False, and the loop terminates cleanly.

The main game loop begins and this is where the core logic of the game resides. The loop is divided into four phases. The first phase handles input from the keyboard, mouse, or game controller.

The second phase is where the game state is updated. This is where you'd typically add logic to move characters, update scores, check for collisions, control timers, or handle other dynamic behavior.

The third phase handles rendering. Before drawing anything new, the screen is cleared with **screen.fill((0, 0, 0))** to erase the previous frame. You can also clear the screen with a background image if you're using one. You then draw all visible game elements here, such as backgrounds, sprites, objects, and user interface components. The call to **pygame.display.flip()** updates the entire screen to show the new frame.

In the final phase, the frame rate is capped using **clock.tick(FPS)** which pauses the loop just long enough to maintain the target frame rate. This ensures the game runs at a predictable speed and prevents it from consuming unnecessary CPU resources. When the game ends, **pygame.quit()** is called to shut down the Pygame modules and exit cleanly.

Chapter 3: Game Windows & Loops

Challenge

Write a Python program using Pygame that demonstrates all the skills you learned in this chapter.

Your program must:

- Import and initialise Pygame.
- Create a display window that is 800 pixels wide and 600 pixels high.
- Give the window a title that appears in the title bar.
- Use a running variable to control a game loop that keeps the program active until the user closes the window.
- Handle the QUIT event so the program exits cleanly when the player clicks the close button.
- Fill the screen with a solid background colour before updating the display each frame.
- Call pygame.quit() after the game loop ends.

Extra Challenges:

- Change the background color by editing the RGB values in your code.
- Change the window size to something other than 800 × 600 and run the program again.
- Change the window title to your own game name.
- Add a **pygame.time.Clock()** object to your program and call **clock.tick(60)** inside the game loop to limit the frame rate to 60 FPS.

When you run your program, a window titled with your chosen caption should appear at 800×600. The client area should display a solid background colour that you redraw every frame.

The application must remain responsive: you should be able to drag the window, focus/unfocus it, and close it using the title-bar close button.

Chapter 3: Game Windows & Loops

When you click close, the program should terminate without any traceback or "Not Responding" behaviour. If you added the optional frame-rate cap with **pygame.time.Clock()**, CPU usage should be modest and the window should feel smooth and predictable.

If you change the RGB values in your code and re-run the program, the background colour changes accordingly.

If you change the window size or title in code, those changes should be reflected immediately on launch.

4 Drawing to the Screen

Once you've created your game window and started your main game loop, the next step is to fill that window with visual elements — backgrounds, characters, objects, text, and effects.

In this chapter, we'll explore how to draw to the screen using Pygame's core tools: surfaces, images, rectangles, and layering.

Note, in the printed book, some lines of code may wrap onto multiple lines due to formatting, but in your code editor they should be typed as a single continuous line.

We've included all the source code for this chapter in the following repository:

elluminetpress.com/pydraw

Chapter 4: Drawing to the Screen

Blitting Images

In Pygame, "drawing" usually means copying one Surface onto another. This is done using a method called blitting (short for bit block transfer). It's how sprites, tiles, and backgrounds are displayed during gameplay. Let's start with a simple example. First, we need a display surface to represent the game window (here we've called it screen):

```
screen = pygame.display.set_mode((800, 600))
```

Next, we load an image into another Surface (here called background):

```
background = pygame.image.load("images/bg.jpg")
```

Finally, we use **screen.blit()** to copy the background Surface onto the display Surface (screen) at position (0, 0):

```
screen.blit(background, (0, 0))
```

Blitting happens during the game loop. After drawing everything, you use **pygame.display.flip()** or **pygame.display.update()** to show the new frame on screen.

Let's take a look at a full example. First, the **Pygame** library is imported. This library provides all the necessary modules for handling graphics, input, sound, and game logic.

```
import pygame
```

Next, the **pygame.init()** function is called to initialize all the Pygame modules that the game will use.

```
pygame.init()
```

Next, we create a display surface—the area where all drawing happens. The dimensions of the screen are set using **screen_width = 800** and **screen_height = 600**. These values are passed to **pygame.display.set_mode()**, which returns a display Surface representing the main game window.

```
screen_width = 800
screen_height = 600
screen = pygame.display.set_mode((screen_width,
                                  screen_height))
```

63

Chapter 4: Drawing to the Screen

To label the window, **pygame.display.set_caption()** is used. This sets the title text that appears in the window's title bar.

```
pygame.display.set_caption("Blitting Example")
```

An image file is then loaded using **pygame.image.load()**. The path to the image file should be correct and relative to the current working directory. The image is loaded into a Surface object (background), which can then be drawn (or "blitted") onto the display surface (screen).

```
background = pygame.image.load("images/bg.jpg")
```

The main loop of the game begins. This loop keeps the window open and running until the player explicitly closes it. A variable named running is set to True, and while this variable remains True, the loop will continue to execute. Inside the loop, all events in the event queue are checked using **pygame.event.get()**. If a QUIT event is detected—such as clicking the close button on the window—the running variable is set to False, which causes the loop to exit.

```
running = True
while running:
    for event in pygame.event.get():
        if event.type == pygame.QUIT:
            running = False
```

Each frame, the background image is drawn to the display surface (screen) using **screen.blit(background, (0, 0))**. The coordinates (0, 0) specify that the image should be drawn starting from the top-left corner of the screen.

```
    screen.blit(background, (0, 0))
```

After all drawing operations for the current frame are completed, the display is updated using **pygame.display.flip()**. This function makes all drawn content visible on the screen.

```
    pygame.display.flip()
```

Once the main loop exits, the program ends by calling **pygame.quit()**. This function uninitializes all Pygame modules.

```
pygame.quit()
```

Chapter 4: Drawing to the Screen

Drawing Shapes

In addition to working with images and sprites, Pygame allows you to draw simple geometric shapes directly onto surfaces. This can be useful for quickly prototyping gameplay elements, creating effects, or adding visual indicators such as health bars, borders, or bullets.

Shapes are drawn using functions from the **pygame.draw** module. These functions render directly onto a surface — typically a display surface called screen — and require parameters such as position, size, and color.

```
pygame.draw.rect(screen, (255, 0, 0), (100, 100, 50, 50))
```

This draws a solid red rectangle at position (100, 100) with a width of 50 pixels and height of 50 pixels. The first argument is the destination display surface (screen), the second is an RGB color tuple (255,0,0), and the third is a rectangle defined by its top-left position and size (100, 100, 50, 50).

You can also draw circles.

```
pygame.draw.circle(screen, (0, 255, 0), (400, 300), 40)
```

The first argument, screen, is the surface we're drawing onto. The second argument, (0, 255, 0), is the color of the circle in RGB format—this one is bright green. The third argument, (400, 300), sets the position of the center of the circle on the screen using x and y coordinates. The final argument, 40, sets the radius of the circle in pixels.

65

Chapter 4: Drawing to the Screen

Or a line. It starts at position (100, 100) and ends at (300, 300)—these are the x and y coordinates for the start and end points of the line. The color (0, 0, 255) defines a solid blue color. The final argument, 5, sets the thickness of the line to 5 pixels.

```
pygame.draw.line(screen, (0, 0, 255), (100, 100),
                                       (300, 300), 5)
```

An ellipse. The last argument is a rectangle tuple (200, 200, 100, 50), defines the bounding box of the ellipse. The top-left corner of the box is at (200, 200), with a width of 100 pixels and a height of 50 pixels. .

```
pygame.draw.ellipse(screen, (255, 255, 0), (200, 200,
                                             100, 50))
```

Adding Text

Text in Pygame is rendered using the **pygame.font** module. Before you can display any text, you must first create a font object and then render your message as a new surface.

Scan for Video

```
font = pygame.font.Font(None, 36)

text_surface = font.render("Hello, Pygame!", True,
                           (255, 255, 255))

screen.blit(text_surface, (50, 50))
```

This code creates a new font of size 36 using the pygame default font (None as the first argument). The **render()** method converts the text string into a Surface using anti-aliasing (True), and the given color. The resulting surface (text_surface) can then be blitted onto the display surface (screen) at a specified position.

In Pygame, you can use both system fonts (installed on your computer) and custom font files (such as .ttf or .otf placed in your project folder).

```
font = pygame.font.SysFont("arial", 32)

font = pygame.font.Font("fonts/custom_font.ttf", 24)
```

Chapter 4: Drawing to the Screen

Surfaces, Rects, and Coordinates

Pygame uses Surfaces as the building blocks for everything visual. A Surface is like a blank canvas you can draw on — it can represent the display Surface for the game window, an image, or even an off-screen area used to construct more complex graphics.

Scan for Video

When you create a game window, Pygame returns the display Surface (stored in a variable called screen in this case):

```
screen = pygame.display.set_mode((width, height))
```

Similarly, when you load an image from a file, Pygame creates a new Surface object containing that image (player1 in this case):

```
player1 = pygame.image.load("images/rocket.png")
```

To manage position and size of your images more efficiently, Pygame uses Rect objects. A Rect object represents a rectangular area defined by position and size, and is typically used to position Surfaces and to handle alignment or collision detection.

When working with images, you can create a Rect object from the surface using the **.get_rect()** method.

```
player1_rect = player1.get_rect()
```

The returned Rect object (player1_rect) has the same width and height as the image surface object and is positioned at the origin (0, 0) by default.

This is illustrated by the red outline in the image on the right.

Chapter 4: Drawing to the Screen

You can then reposition it by modifying attributes such as .topleft, .x, .y, or .center. For example:

```
player1_rect.topleft = (100, 150)
```

This sets the top-left corner of the Rect object to coordinates (100, 150), positioning it 100 pixels from the left edge of the screen and 150 pixels from the top. This method is useful for initial placement.

Alternatively, you can use .x and .y. In a Rect object, these represent the x and y coordinates of the top-left corner individually:

```
player1_rect.x += 5    # Move right
player1_rect.y -= 5    # Move up
```

They provide direct access to the same values as .topleft, but allow you to adjust the horizontal and vertical positions separately. This makes them particularly useful for movement during gameplay.

Chapter 4: Drawing to the Screen

We can use other attributes depending on how we want to align the object. For example, the **.center** attribute positions the Rect based on its center point rather than its corner:

Once your positioning is set, you draw the image onto the display surface (screen) using the **.blit()** method. This copies the player1 surface onto the display surface (screen) at the location specified by player1_rect.

```
screen.blit(player1, player1_rect)
```

To make the image appear on the display, you must then update the game window with:

```
pygame.display.flip()
```

Understanding how surfaces and Rect objects work together is essential for building any game in Pygame.

Surfaces handle the visual content, while Rects control positioning, alignment, and collision boundaries. Once you're comfortable manipulating these, you'll be able to place, move, and animate sprites anywhere on the screen.

As you move forward, try experimenting with different Rect attributes and surface transformations to build more dynamic and interactive scenes.

Using Colors

In Pygame, colors are represented using the RGB color model. RGB stands for Red, Green, and Blue — the three primary colors of light.

Chapter 4: Drawing to the Screen

By mixing these in different amounts, you can create any color you need for your game.

An RGB color is defined as a tuple of three integers, each ranging from 0 to 255:

```
(red_value, green_value, blue_value)
```

For example

```
(255, 0, 0)         # Red
(0, 255, 0)         # Green
(0, 0, 255)         # Blue
(255, 255, 255)     # White
(0, 0, 0)           # Black
(128, 128, 128)     # Gray
```

The first number controls the intensity of red, the second controls green, and the third controls blue. A value of 0 means none of that color, while 255 means full intensity. You can mix them together to create custom colors — for example, (255, 255, 0) creates yellow (full red + full green, no blue).

Here's an example

```
import pygame
pygame.init()

screen = pygame.display.set_mode((800, 600))
pygame.display.set_caption("Using Colors Example")

running = True
while running:
    for event in pygame.event.get():
        if event.type == pygame.QUIT:
            running = False

    screen.fill((0, 0, 255))
    pygame.draw.rect(screen, (255, 0, 0), (50, 50, 100, 50))
    pygame.draw.circle(screen, (0, 255, 0), (400, 300), 40)

    pygame.display.flip()

pygame.quit()
```

Chapter 4: Drawing to the Screen

Challenge

Write a Python program using Pygame that does the following:

- Import and initialize Pygame.

- Create a display window 800 × 600.

- Set a window title of your choice.

- Load a background image and blit it to the top-left corner each frame.

- Load a sprite image (e.g., a character or object), create a Rect from it, and position it somewhere on the screen.

- Draw at least two shapes (rectangle, circle, line, or ellipse) directly onto the screen surface.

- Display some text using either the default system font or a font file, and blit it to the screen.

- Use a game loop that:

    - Processes the event queue.

    - Handles the QUIT event so the program exits cleanly when the window is closed.

    - Draws the background, sprite, shapes, and text every frame.

    - Calls **pygame.display.flip()** to update the screen.

- Call **pygame.quit()** after the game loop ends.

Make sure your images are in the correct folders images/bg.jpg and images/ufo.png.

bg.jpg

rocket.png

ufo.png

5

Sprites & Movement

Now that you've learned how to draw images and shapes to the screen, it's time to bring them to life. In this chapter, we'll explore how to control your player character, move objects around the screen, and detect when things collide — a vital part of gameplay in nearly every genre, from platformers to shooters.

Note, in the printed book, some lines of code may wrap onto multiple lines due to formatting, but in your code editor they should be typed as a single continuous line.

We've included all the source code for this chapter in the following repository:

elluminetpress.com/pysprites

Chapter 5: Sprites, Movement, & Collision Detection

Creating Player & Enemy Objects

A sprite is a visual object that moves independently on the screen — like a player, an enemy, a bullet, or a coin. In Pygame, a sprite typically includes:

- An image or surface that represents how it looks
- A Rect that tracks where it is
- Some logic to move or update it

Let's have a look at a simple example. Before using any Pygame features, you must import the library and initialise it:

```
import pygame
pygame.init()
```

Next, define the size of the game window and open it:

```
screen_width = 800
screen_height = 600
screen    =   pygame.display.set_mode((screen_width,
                                        screen_height))
pygame.display.set_caption("Player and Enemy Demo")
```

Now load the player and enemy images into surface objects. Here **.convert_alpha()** preserves transparency, which is essential for clean visuals in sprite-based games.

```
player_image = pygame.image.load("images/p1.png").
                                        convert_alpha()
enemy_image  = pygame.image.load("images/e1.png").
                                        convert_alpha()
```

Every sprite needs a position on the screen. This is handled using a Rect — a rectangle object that stores the sprite's size and coordinates.

```
player_rect = player_image.get_rect()
enemy_rect = enemy_image.get_rect()
```

When you call **.get_rect()** on a surface like **player_image**, Pygame creates a Rect object with the same size as the image — and sets its default position to (0, 0) (the top-left corner of the screen).

Chapter 5: Sprites, Movement, & Collision Detection

Next, we set their initial positions on the screen using the topleft attribute.

```
player_rect.topleft = (100, 300)
enemy_rect.topleft = (500, 300)
```

This places the top-left corner of the sprite at the specified (x, y) position.

Next, we start the game loop. This keeps your game running, checking for input and drawing updates.

```
running = True
while running:
    for event in pygame.event.get():
        if event.type == pygame.QUIT:
            running = False
```

To make the game display objects correctly on the screen, we must redraw everything during each frame of the game loop. This line fills the entire screen with a solid color — in this case, black. The tuple (0, 0, 0) represents the RGB values for black, where red, green, and blue are all set to zero.

```
    screen.fill((0, 0, 0))
```

Next we draw the player sprite onto the screen. The **blit()** function stands for block image transfer, and it is used to copy an surface onto another surface — in this case, the player image surface onto the display surface (screen).

Chapter 5: Sprites, Movement, & Collision Detection

The **player_image** is the Surface object representing the player's appearance, and **player_rect** is a Rect object that tells Pygame where to place the image on the screen. By separating the image and its position, we can easily move the player later by updating the **player_rect** while keeping the visual asset the same.

```
screen.blit(player_image, player_rect)
screen.blit(enemy_image, enemy_rect)
```

After all drawing commands are finished, this following line updates the display so the player can see the current frame. Internally, Pygame uses double buffering — all drawing happens off-screen until you call **flip()** at which point the completed frame is shown all at once. This eliminates flickering and ensures a smooth display. Without this step, the screen would not update, and none of your drawn objects would be visible to the player.

```
pygame.display.flip()
```

After the game loop ends, quit Pygame.

```
pygame.quit()
```

Keyboard Events in Pygame

Let's make the previous program interactive. We can do this by making the player character move around the screen using the arrow keys.

When the game is running, input needs to be constantly monitored. This is done using an event queue. Pygame provides this through **pygame.event.get()** which collects all recent input events (keyboard, mouse, system messages).

This example checks for the QUIT event (such as when the player closes the window) and ends the game loop.

```
for event in pygame.event.get():
    if event.type == pygame.QUIT:
        running = False
```

To handle keyboard input, you can respond to key press events like this:

Chapter 5: Sprites, Movement, & Collision Detection

```
if event.type == pygame.KEYDOWN:
    if event.key == pygame.K_SPACE:
        print("Space bar pressed")
```

This is how your game becomes interactive — you can fire projectiles, pause the game, and more based on input.

You can detect key presses using the KEYDOWN and KEYUP events along with specific constants for each key.

```
for event in pygame.event.get():
    if event.type == pygame.KEYDOWN:
        if event.key == pygame.K_SPACE:
            ...
        if event.key == pygame.K_ESCAPE:
            ...
```

You can use any of the following key constants in your event handling code to detect when specific keys are pressed or released.

Constant	Key
pygame.K_SPACE	Space bar
pygame.K_RETURN	Enter / Return
pygame.K_ESCAPE	Escape
pygame.K_LEFT	Left Arrow
pygame.K_RIGHT	Right Arrow
pygame.K_UP	Up Arrow
pygame.K_DOWN	Down Arrow
pygame.K_a – K_z	Letter keys
pygame.K_0 – K_9	Number keys
pygame.K_TAB	Tab
pygame.K_BACKSPACE	Backspace
pygame.K_LCTRL	Left Control
pygame.K_LSHIFT	Left Shift

Chapter 5: Sprites, Movement, & Collision Detection

For continuous movement — like holding down the arrow keys to move a player — you should use **pygame.key.get_pressed()**. This checks the current state of all keys and returns a list of boolean values. These are commonly used in games to control movement, especially for player characters. (e.g., holding down a key to keep moving).

```
keys = pygame.key.get_pressed()
if keys[pygame.K_LEFT]:
    player_x -= player_speed
if keys[pygame.K_RIGHT]:
    player_x += player_speed
if keys[pygame.K_UP]:
    player_y -= player_speed
if keys[pygame.K_DOWN]:
    player_y += player_speed
```

Now let's put it all together by writing a simple program that creates a game window, processes input, and remains open until the player chooses to close it. Before using any Pygame features, we import the library and initialise it.

```
import pygame
pygame.init()
```

This creates the main game window, which is 800 pixels wide and 600 pixels tall. It returns a surface object where all your game visuals will be drawn.

```
screen = pygame.display.set_mode((800, 600))
pygame.display.set_caption("Interactive Window")
```

Next, we need to control the frame rate of the game, otherwise it will run too quickly. We do this by creating a clock object. This ensures the game runs smoothly and at a consistent speed across all systems.

```
clock = pygame.time.Clock()
```

Loads an image file for the player character and converts it into a Pygame surface object.

```
player_image = pygame.image.load("images/p1.png").
                            convert_alpha()
```

77

Chapter 5: Sprites, Movement, & Collision Detection

Create a Rect object the same size as the player image. This tracks the player's position and makes it easier to move or detect collisions.

```
player_rect = player_image.get_rect()
```

Sets the top-left corner of the player's rectangle to position (400, 300) on the screen. This defines where the player will appear when the game starts.

```
player_rect.topleft = (400, 300)
```

Define how many pixels the player moves with each key press. Increasing this number makes the character move faster.

```
player_speed = 5
```

Start the game loop. This keeps your game running, checking for input and drawing updates.

```
running = True
while running:
```

Handle key press events for spacebar using the event queue. This is for keys that a pressed once. We'll just add a line to print a message to the console at this stage.

```
    for event in pygame.event.get():
        if event.type == pygame.QUIT:
            running = False
        elif event.type == pygame.KEYDOWN:
            if event.key == pygame.K_SPACE:
                print("Space bar pressed")
            if event.key == pygame.K_ESCAPE:
                print("Escape key pressed")
```

Now for the arrow keys. Since these are often held down to move the player character, we don't use the event queue as above, we check the key state instead.

```
    keys = pygame.key.get_pressed()
```

If the left arrow key is held, the player's horizontal position (x) is decreased, moving them left across the screen.

```
    if keys[pygame.K_LEFT]:
```

Chapter 5: Sprites, Movement, & Collision Detection

```
    player_rect.x -= player_speed
```

If the right arrow key is held, the player moves to the right by increasing the x-position.

```
    if keys[pygame.K_RIGHT]:
        player_rect.x += player_speed
```

If the up arrow key is held, the player moves upward by reducing the vertical position (y).

```
    if keys[pygame.K_UP]:
        player_rect.y -= player_speed
```

If the down arrow key is held, the player moves downward by increasing the y-position.

```
    if keys[pygame.K_DOWN]:
        player_rect.y += player_speed
```

Once we're done updating positions and handling input, we fill the entire screen with black before drawing anything else. This clears the previous frame and prevents visual glitches or ghosting effects.

```
    screen.fill((30, 30, 30))
```

Draws the player image at the position specified by player_rect. This makes the player appear at their updated location each frame.

```
    screen.blit(player_image, player_rect)
```

Updates the screen with everything that's been drawn this frame. Without this, nothing would be visible. It also ensures smooth visuals using double-buffering.

```
    pygame.display.flip()
```

Pauses the loop briefly to maintain a consistent 60 frames per second. This keeps animations and gameplay running at the right speed on different computers.

```
    clock.tick(60)

pygame.quit()
```

Chapter 5: Sprites, Movement, & Collision Detection

Game Controllers

Game controllers, gamepads and joysticks are fully supported in Pygame via its **pygame.joystick** module, which allows you to use physical controllers like Xbox, PlayStation, or generic a USB controller such as the one pictured below.

For this particular controller, buttons are discrete inputs, meaning they return 0 (not pressed) or 1 (pressed). Each physical button on the controller is mapped to a numbered index.

On the left control stick, Axis 0 is left-right movement. This corresponds to the left analog stick's horizontal movement. Pushing the stick left returns a float close to -1.0, right returns +1.0, and the center (neutral) position is around 0.0.

80

Chapter 5: Sprites, Movement, & Collision Detection

Axis 1 is up-down movement. This corresponds to the left analog stick's vertical movement. Upward movement is typically -1.0, downward is +1.0, and resting position is around 0.0. Not all controllers map the controls in this way. I have included **controllertest.py** to help you map your controller.

Let's take a look at an example. First, we need to import all the libraries we're going to use in the program.

```
import pygame
import sys
```

Then initialise pygame

```
pygame.init()
```

The line **pygame.joystick.init()** specifically enables joystick or game controller support. This setup allows us to access connected USB controllers. Optional if **pygame.init()** is used.

```
pygame.joystick.init()
```

Next, we check if any controllers are connected using pygame.**joystick.get_count()**. If no controllers are detected, we print a message and exit the program early with **sys.exit()** to avoid errors later.

```
if pygame.joystick.get_count() == 0:
    print("No controller detected.")
    sys.exit()
```

If a controller is detected, we connect to the first one using pygame.**joystick.Joystick(0)** and then call **joystick.init()** to activate it. The line **print(f"Using controller: {joystick.get_name()}")** outputs the name of the connected controller to confirm it's been recognized by the program.

```
joystick = pygame.joystick.Joystick(0)
joystick.init()
print(f"Using controller: {joystick.get_name()}")
```

Next, we create our game window as normal and give the window a title.

```
screen = pygame.display.set_mode((800, 600))
pygame.display.set_caption("Controller Example")
```

Chapter 5: Sprites, Movement, & Collision Detection

To control the game's speed, we use pygame.time.Clock() to create a clock object, which allows us to cap the frame rate later on.

```
clock = pygame.time.Clock()
```

Next, we load the player's sprite image using **pygame.image.load()** and call **.convert_alpha()** to enable transparency support.

```
player_image = pygame.image.load("images/p1.png").convert_alpha()
```

We then create a Rect object from the image using **get_rect()** to manage the player's position and size, and position it on screen with **player_rect.topleft = (400, 300)**.

```
player_rect = player_image.get_rect()
player_rect.topleft = (400, 300)
```

A **player_speed** variable is also defined, which controls how fast the player moves across the screen.

```
player_speed = 5
```

Start the game loop. This keeps your game running, checking for input and drawing updates.

```
running = True
while running:
```

Start the event loop and check If the player closes the window (a QUIT event), we set running = False to exit the loop.

```
    for event in pygame.event.get():
        if event.type == pygame.QUIT:
            running = False
```

Next we need to check for button presses on the controller. We do this by checking for a **JOYBUTTONDOWN** event.

```
        elif event.type == pygame.JOYBUTTONDOWN:
            if event.button == 0:
                print("Button 0 pressed")
            elif event.button == 1:
                print("Button 1 pressed")
```

Chapter 5: Sprites, Movement, & Collision Detection

Movement is handled by reading analog stick values with **joystick.get_axis(0)** for the horizontal axis (X) and **joystick.get_axis(1)** for the vertical axis (Y). These return float values from -1.0 to +1.0, which we multiply by **player_speed** to determine how far the player moves.

```
x_axis = joystick.get_axis(0)
y_axis = joystick.get_axis(1)
```

We also add a deadzone check (abs(x_axis) > 0.1) to avoid drift caused by slight stick movement when it's meant to be idle. This is because you might get something like 0.03 or -0.06 even when the stick appears at rest. If you don't account for this, your game character might constantly drift or jitter without user input.

```
if abs(x_axis) > 0.1:
    player_rect.x += int(x_axis * player_speed)
if abs(y_axis) > 0.1:
    player_rect.y += int(y_axis * player_speed)
```

Once we're done updating positions and handling input, we fill the entire screen with black before drawing anything else. This clears the previous frame and prevents visual glitches or ghosting effects.

```
screen.fill((30, 30, 30))
```

Draws the player image at the position specified by player_rect. This makes the player appear at their updated location each frame.

```
screen.blit(player_image, player_rect)
```

Updates the screen with everything that's been drawn this frame. Without this, nothing would be visible. It also ensures smooth visuals using double-buffering.

```
pygame.display.flip()
```

Pauses the loop briefly to maintain a consistent 60 frames per second.

```
clock.tick(60)
```

```
pygame.quit()
```

Chapter 5: Sprites, Movement, & Collision Detection

Collision Detection

Collision detection is how a game knows when two things touch — whether it's a ball hitting a brick, a spaceship firing a laser, or a player running into a wall. Without collision detection, objects would pass through each other like ghosts, and your game wouldn't feel interactive or responsive.

In Pygame collisions are checked using Rect objects. These act like invisible boxes that surround each image.

They don't care about the fine details of an image (like a character's shape or transparency); instead, they only look at whether the bounding boxes overlap.

Games need to check for collisions constantly — usually every single frame — to stay interactive. In Pygame, this is handled using simple, built-in methods like **.colliderect()**, which tells you if one Rect is overlapping another.

Let's take a look at a simple example. Here, we have a program that turns a square green once a collision is detected. Before using any Pygame features, we import the library and initialise it.

```
import pygame

pygame.init()
```

Next, we create our game window as normal and give the window a title.

```
screen = pygame.display.set_mode((800, 600))

pygame.display.set_caption("Collision Example")
```

Chapter 5: Sprites, Movement, & Collision Detection

To control the game's speed, we use pygame.time.Clock() to create a clock object, which allows us to cap the frame rate later on.

```
clock = pygame.time.Clock()
```

Next, we load the player's sprite image using **pygame.image.load()** and call **.convert_alpha()** to enable transparency support.

```
player_image  =  pygame.image.load("images/p1.png")
                                            .convert_alpha()
```

We then create a Rect object from the image using **get_rect()** to manage the player's position and size, and position it on screen with **player_rect.topleft = (400, 300)**.

```
player_rect = player_image.get_rect()
player_rect.topleft = (100, 300)
```

Next, we create the enemy object as a plain-colored square rather than loading an image. We make a new 80×80-pixel transparent Surface using **pygame.Surface()** with the SRCALPHA flag for per-pixel transparency. We fill it with a solid red color using **fill((255, 0, 0))**. Then we generate its Rect using **.get_rect()** and position it at (500, 300) using **topleft**.

```
enemy_image  =  pygame.Surface((80,  80),  pygame
                                            .SRCALPHA)
enemy_image.fill((255, 0, 0))
enemy_rect = enemy_image.get_rect()
enemy_rect.topleft = (500, 300)
```

We define a variable **player_speed** to control how fast the player moves across the screen. This is the number of pixels the player will move per frame when a direction key is held down.

```
player_speed = 5
```

Start the game loop. This keeps your game running, checking for input and drawing updates.

```
running = True

while running:
```

Chapter 5: Sprites, Movement, & Collision Detection

Start the event loop and check If the player closes the window (a QUIT event), we set running = False to exit the loop.

```
for event in pygame.event.get():
    if event.type == pygame.QUIT:
        running = False
```

We check for real-time keyboard input using **pygame.key.get_pressed()**, which returns a list of Boolean values indicating which keys are currently being held down. If the player holds an arrow key, we adjust the corresponding coordinate of **player_rect** by the **player_speed**. This moves the player left, right, up, or down accordingly.

```
keys = pygame.key.get_pressed()
if keys[pygame.K_LEFT]:
    player_rect.x -= player_speed
if keys[pygame.K_RIGHT]:
    player_rect.x += player_speed
if keys[pygame.K_UP]:
    player_rect.y -= player_speed
if keys[pygame.K_DOWN]:
    player_rect.y += player_speed
```

Next, we check for a collision between the player and the enemy using the **.colliderect()** method, which checks whether the two Rect objects overlap (**player_rect** and **enemy_rect**). If they do, we change the enemy's color to green to indicate a hit. If they don't, we reset the enemy's color back to red.

```
if player_rect.colliderect(enemy_rect):
    enemy_image.fill((0, 255, 0))
else:
    enemy_image.fill((255, 0, 0))
```

Once we're done updating positions, handling input, and checking for collisions, we fill the entire screen with black before drawing anything else. This clears the previous frame and prevents visual glitches or ghosting effects.

```
screen.fill((30, 30, 30))
```

We then draw both the player and enemy images at their current positions using **blit()**.

Chapter 5: Sprites, Movement, & Collision Detection

This copies each image Surface to the screen Surface at the position defined by their respective Rect objects.

```
screen.blit(player_image, player_rect)
screen.blit(enemy_image, enemy_rect)
```

To finish the frame, we call pygame.display.flip() to update the display and show the latest frame. Pygame uses double buffering internally, so all drawing happens off-screen until this point.

```
pygame.display.flip()
```

We call **clock.tick(60)** to pause the loop just long enough to maintain a maximum of 60 frames per second. This keeps movement smooth and consistent across different machines.

```
clock.tick(60)
```

Finally, after the loop exits, we call **pygame.quit()** to cleanly shut down all Pygame modules and close the window.

pygame.quit()

When you run the program, you'll see the square turn from red to green when your player moves over it.

Chapter 5: Sprites, Movement, & Collision Detection

Animations

Animation in Pygame involves displaying a series of images (or frames) in a rapid sequence to create the illusion of motion.

To create an animation, you need a series of images. These frames can be loaded from an image file such as PNG using the **pygame.image.load()** function. You can load the frames individually or from a directory using functions like **os.listdir()** to iterate over the files. If you have lots of frames it makes sense to load them from a directory.

To keep things simple, we are going to load four frames individually so you can see how the process works. The following loads the png images and places them in a list called **image_sprite**.

```
image_sprite = [pygame.image.load("frame01.png"),
                pygame.image.load("frame02.png"),
                pygame.image.load("frame03.png"),
                pygame.image.load("frame04.png")]
```

Once you've loaded your image frames into a list, the next step is to animate them — that is, to cycle through the images over time to create the illusion of motion. This is done by changing the image that's drawn to the screen on a timed basis.

Let's start by setting up a few variables to manage this. These are declared before the main game loop begins:

```
frame_index = 0
animation_timer = 0
animation_speed = 150  # milliseconds between frames
```

The **frame_index** variable keeps track of which frame should be displayed. Initially, it is set to 0, which corresponds to the first image in the list. The **animation_timer** will accumulate time between frames, and **animation_speed** defines how long each frame should be displayed before switching to the next — in this case, 150 milliseconds.

```
clock = pygame.time.Clock()
```

Inside the main game loop, we call **clock.tick(60)** once per frame.

Chapter 5: Sprites, Movement, & Collision Detection

This limits the loop to approximately 60 iterations (frames) per second and returns the number of milliseconds that have passed since the previous call to tick().

```
frame_time = clock.tick(60)
```

The next line adds the amount of time that has passed since the last frame (**frame_time**) to the **animation_timer**. It keeps a running total of how much time has accumulated, so the program can track when it's time to change to the next animation frame.

```
animation_timer += frame_time
```

Next we need to check if enough time has passed to show the next animation frame. If **animation_timer** is greater than or equal to **animation_speed**, that means the current frame has been on screen long enough. The line **animation_timer %= animation_speed** keeps any extra time that went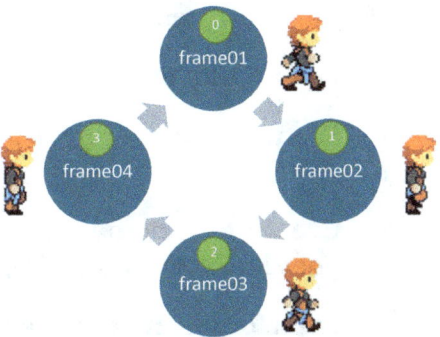
over. For example, if the timer reached 160 but the frame only needed 150 milliseconds, it keeps the leftover 10. That leftover time helps keep the animation running smoothly and on time. Then, **frame_index = (frame_index + 1) % len(image_sprite)** moves to the next frame in the list.

```
if animation_timer >= animation_speed:
   animation_timer %= animation_speed
   frame_index = (frame_index + 1) % len(image_sprite)
```

Now that we know which frame to display, we draw it to the screen. Here, the current frame image is drawn to the top-left corner of the screen at position (0, 0). In this version of the program, we're not moving the sprite — we're simply animating it in place by cycling through frames at a fixed interval.

```
screen.blit(image_sprite[frame_index], (0, 0))
```

The final step in the loop is to update the display so the new frame becomes visible:

```
pygame.display.flip()
```

Chapter 5: Sprites, Movement, & Collision Detection

Challenge

Write a Python program using Pygame that does the following:

1. Window and Setup
   - Import and initialize Pygame.
   - Create an 800 × 600 display window and set a window title.
   - Create clock to cap the frame rate at 60 FPS.

2. Player and Enemy
   - Load a player image .
   - Create a Rect from the player image and position it at (100, 300).
   - Create an enemy as a red square and get its Rect and position it at (500, 300).
   - Load four frames into a list named image_sprite: "frame01.png", "frame02.png", "frame03.png", "frame04.png".
   - Use this to animate the player.

3. Keyboard Input (Continuous)
   - Move the player's Rect with the arrow keys.
   - Use a variable to control movement speed.

4. Collision Detection
   - Each frame, check for collision.
   - If colliding, make the enemy square green; otherwise keep it red.

5. Drawing and Presentation
   - Each frame: clear the screen, then blit the animation, and the enemy.
   - Handle the QUIT event after the loop ends.

Chapter 5: Sprites, Movement, & Collision Detection

You'll should end up with something like this. You will be able to move the player around the screen. The square will turn green when there is a collision.

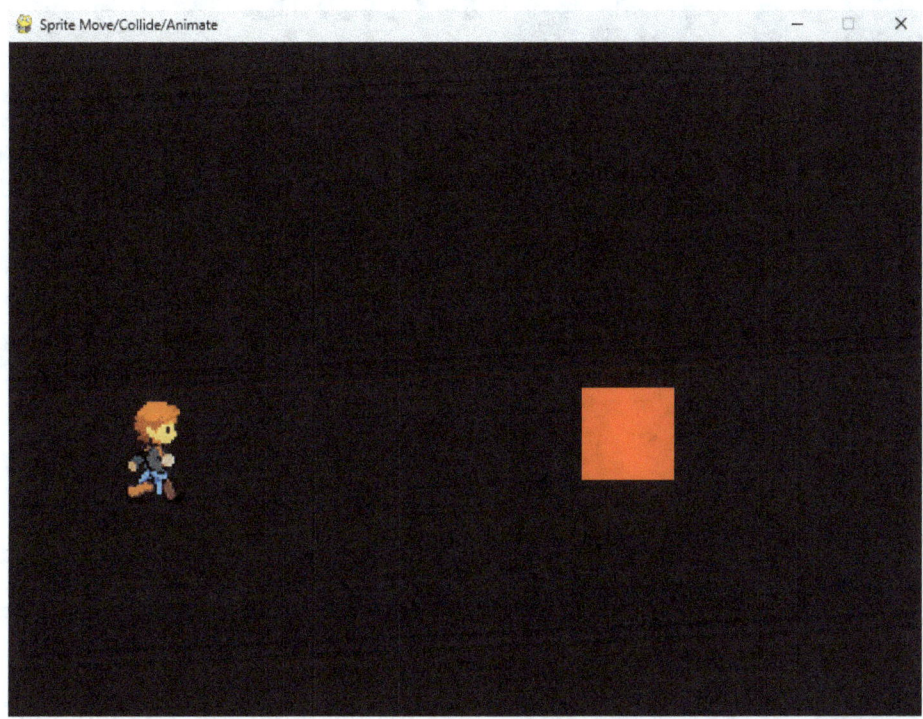

As an additional challenge, make the red enemy square patrol horizontally.

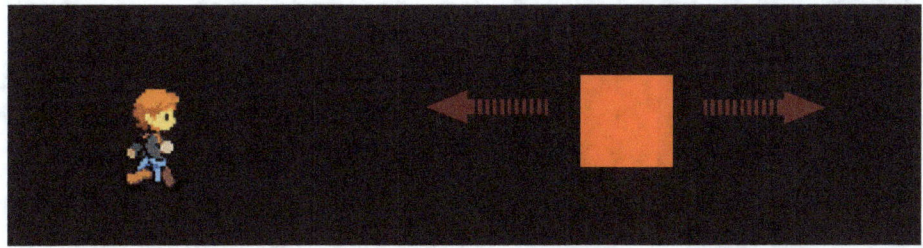

Use an enemy_speed and a direction variable (e.g., enemy_dir = 1 or -1).

Each frame, move the enemy along x.

Reverse direction when its Rect touches the left or right edge of the window.

6 Sound & Music

Sound is a powerful part of game design. It adds atmosphere, reinforces actions, and provides feedback to the player. Even a short sound effect — like a laser blast or jump noise — can make gameplay feel more responsive and engaging.

Pygame includes a dedicated audio module called **pygame.mixer**, which is responsible for handling all sound playback. This includes both short sound effects (like shooting or collisions) and background music.

Note, in the printed book, some lines of code may wrap onto multiple lines due to formatting, but in your code editor they should be typed as a single continuous line.

We've included all the source code for this chapter in the following repository:

elluminetpress.com/pymusic

Chapter 6: Sound & Music

Initializing the Mixer

Before you can play sounds, you need to initialize the mixer. This sets up the audio system. You can also pass arguments to control things like sample rate and buffer size, but the defaults are usually fine for most 2D games.

```
pygame.mixer.init()
```

After the mixer is initialized, you can load sound files using **pygame.mixer.Sound()** for short effects or **pygame.mixer.music** for longer tracks like background music.

Loading and Playing Sound Effects

Sound effects (like jumping, shooting, or collisions) are typically short .wav or .mp3 files. You load them using **pygame.mixer.Sound()**

```
fire_sound = pygame.mixer.Sound("sounds/laser.mp3")
```

We can then play the sound using **.play()**

```
fire_sound.play()
```

Here in the example, I've loaded the **laser.mp3** sound effect to the **rocket.py** program using **pygame.mixer.Sound()**. I've highlighted the lines in bold.

```
import pygame
pygame.init()
pygame.mixer.init()

screen_width = 800
screen_height = 600

screen   =   pygame.display.set_mode((screen_width,
                                    screen_height))
pygame.display.set_caption("Rocket Fire")
player1 = pygame.image.load("images/rocket.png")
player1_rect = player1.get_rect()

fire_sound = pygame.mixer.Sound("audio/laser.mp3")
```

93

Chapter 6: Sound & Music

In event handler inside the game loop, I've added the line so the sound effect plays when you press the space bar. I've highlighted the line in bold.

```
running = True
while running:
        for event in pygame.event.get():
        if event.type == pygame.QUIT:
            running = False
        if event.type == pygame.KEYDOWN:
            if event.key == pygame.K_SPACE:
                fire_sound.play()
    player1_rect.topleft = (100, 150)
    screen.blit(player1, player1_rect)

    pygame.display.flip()
pygame.quit()
```

Background Music

Use **pygame.mixer.music** for longer audio tracks, like looping background music.

```
pygame.mixer.music.load("audio/music.mp3")
```

You can set the volume. The range is from 0.0 (completely silent) to 1.0 (full volume).

```
pygame.mixer.music.set_volume(0.5)
```

You can also control how you want the music to play using arguments with **pygame.mixer.music.play()**. By default, music plays once and stops. However, you can set it to repeat any number of times or loop indefinitely.

```
pygame.mixer.music.play(-1)
```

For example **.play(0)** plays it once **.play(1)** plays it twice (once plus one repeat), and **.play(-1)** loops it forever — which is ideal for background music during gameplay.

Chapter 6: Sound & Music

You can also pause, resume, or stop playback at any time using pause(), unpause(), and stop() respectively.

```
pygame.mixer.music.pause()
```

```
pygame.mixer.music.unpause()
```

```
pygame.mixer.music.stop()
```

Challenge

Write a Python program using Pygame that:

1. Import and initialize Pygame.
2. Initialize the mixer.
3. Create an 800 × 600 display window and set a window title.
4. Load a player sprite (e.g., "images/rocket.png") and position it at (400, 300).
5. Load two different sound effects:
6. One for moving left ("audio/left.wav").
7. One for moving right ("audio/right.wav").
8. Load a background music track (e.g., "audio/music.mp3") and set it to loop continuously at volume 0.5.
9. When the left arrow key is pressed, move the player 20 pixels to the left and play the left-movement sound effect.
10. When the right arrow key is pressed, move the player 20 pixels to the right and play the right-movement sound effect.
11. The background music should play the entire time the program is running.
12. Keep the window open until the player closes it.
13. Handle the QUIT event to exit cleanly and stop the music.

7 Simple Shooter

In this project, you'll create a fast-paced single-screen arcade shooter using Pygame. The player controls a rocket that moves left and right along the bottom of the screen and fires bullets upward to hit a moving UFO. This project introduces interaction between moving sprites, collision detection using Rect objects, sound effects, and image rendering.

Note, in the printed book, some lines of code may wrap onto multiple lines due to formatting, but in your code editor they should be typed as a single continuous line.

We've included all the source code for this chapter in the projects section of the following repository:

elluminetpress.com/pygames

You'll find the final game code listing as simpleshooter.py

Chapter 7: Simple Shooter

Game Description

The player rocket is positioned near the bottom of the screen and can be moved horizontally using the arrow keys. Pressing the space bar fires a bullet upward. A UFO moves horizontally back and forth across the top of the screen. If a bullet hits the UFO, an explosion is displayed and a sound is played. The UFO resets to its original position, ready for the next shot.

Requirements

Before we start coding, it's essential to define exactly what the game must do and the conditions it must meet.

These are separated into two categories: functional requirements, which describe the specific actions and features the game must perform, and non-functional requirements, which define performance standards, quality attributes, and technical constraints.

By outlining these early, we create a clear target for the design and implementation phases.

97

Chapter 7: Simple Shooter

Functional

These describe what the game must do — the specific behaviours and features.

1. The player controls a rocket positioned at the bottom of the screen that can move left and right.
2. The rocket must stay within the left and right edges of the screen.
3. Pressing the space bar fires a bullet straight upward from the rocket's nose.
4. Only one bullet can be active at a time.
5. A UFO moves sideways near the top of the screen, reversing direction when it reaches the left or right edge.
   - If the bullet hits the UFO:
   - Play a "hit" sound.
   - Show an explosion for a short period.
6. Reset the UFO to its starting position.
7. Background music plays in a loop during the game.
8. A "fire" sound plays when the player shoots.

Non-Functional

These describe the quality attributes and constraints for the game.

1. The game should run at a smooth 60 frames per second.
2. The game should exit cleanly when the player closes the window.
3. All images and sounds must load successfully at the start of the game without causing delays during play.
4. The game window size must remain fixed at 800×600 pixels during play.
5. The game's controls should respond instantly to player input without noticeable lag.

Chapter 7: Simple Shooter

Assets

You need the following image and audio files stored in the correct folders so the code can load them successfully. All file names in the code are case-sensitive.

```
Simpleshooter/
├── images/
│   ├── rocket.png
│   ├── bullet.png
│   ├── ufo.png
│   └── explosion.png
├── audio/
│   ├── gamemusic.mp3
│   ├── fire.mp3
│   └── hit.mp3
└── simpleshooter.py
```

Design

Here we decide how the game will be organised before we start writing the code.

When the game starts, it loads all images and sounds once so they are ready to use. The rocket begins in the middle at the bottom of the screen. The bullet starts at the rocket's nose but stays still until fired. The UFO starts near the top and moves sideways. The explosion image is hidden until needed.

We use Pygame Rect objects for the rocket, bullet, UFO, and explosion. A Rect stores an object's position and size. It also lets us easily check if two objects have collided — whether the bullet Rect object overlaps the UFO Rect object.

So each part of the program works like this:

1. Setup – Create the game window, set the frame rate, load all images and sounds, and set the starting positions of the rocket, bullet, UFO, and explosion.

2. Game loop

Chapter 7: Simple Shooter

- Check for input events (movement keys, firing the bullet, quitting the game).
- Update positions:
  - Rocket moves left/right but stays within the screen.
  - UFO moves sideways and turns around at the edges.
  - Bullet moves upward if fired, and disappears if it leaves the screen.
- Check for collisions: if the bullet hits the UFO, play the hit sound, show the explosion for a short time, reset the UFO, and reset the bullet.
- Draw all objects in the correct order and show the updated frame.

3. End game – When the player closes the window, stop the loop, close Pygame, and exit cleanly.

Now we can write what part of the game needs to do using pseudocode. Pseudocode is not real code — it's a way of writing out the steps of a program in plain, easy-to-understand language, without worrying about the exact Python syntax. So we write the steps each part of the program needs to take.

```
1.   SETUP:
         Initialise Pygame
         Create game window (800 x 600)
         Set target frame rate to 60 FPS
         Load images: rocket, bullet, UFO, explosion
         Load sounds: bg music, fire sound, hit sound
         Play background music in a loop
         Create Rect for rocket at bottom of screen
         Create Rect for bullet at rocket's nose
         Create Rect for UFO near top of screen
         Create Rect for explosion (hidden)
         Set bullet as inactive
         Set UFO speed
         Set explosion timer to zero
```

Chapter 7: Simple Shooter

```
2.  GAME LOOP:
        WHILE game is running:
            CHECK for events:
            IF quit event or Escape key pressed:
                End the game
            IF left arrow key is pressed:
                Move rocket left
            IF right arrow key is pressed:
                Move rocket right
            IF space bar AND bullet inactive:
                Position bullet at rocket's nose
                Mark bullet as active
                Play fire sound
            KEEP rocket inside screen bounds
            MOVE UFO horizontally by its speed
            IF UFO reaches left or right edge:
                Reverse UFO direction

            IF bullet is active:
                Move bullet upward
                IF bullet leaves top of screen:
                    Mark bullet as inactive

            IF bullet active AND collide with UFO:
                Play hit sound
                Show explosion at UFO position
                Reset explosion timer
                Mark bullet as inactive
                Reset bullet to rocket's nose
                Reset UFO to starting position

            IF explosion is showing on screen:
                Increase explosion timer
                IF explosion timer greater than limit:
                    Hide explosion

        CLEAR the screen
        DRAW rocket
        DRAW UFO
        IF bullet is active:
            DRAW bullet
        IF explosion is showing:
```

Chapter 7: Simple Shooter

```
        DRAW explosion
        UPDATE display
```

3. END:
```
        Stop background music
        Quit Pygame
        Exit program
```

Implementation

Now that we have the pseudocode, we can use it to start implementing it using Python. We write the actual Python code for each line in the pseudocode listing.

1. SETUP: Import & Initialise Pygame

```
import pygame

pygame.init()
```

Create game window (800 x 600)

```
screen = pygame.display.set_mode((800, 600))

pygame.display.set_caption("Simple Shooter")
```

Set target frame rate to 60 FPS

```
clock = pygame.time.Clock()
```

Load images: rocket, bullet, UFO, explosion

```
rocket_img = pygame.image.load("images/rocket.png").convert_alpha()

bullet_img = pygame.image.load("images/bullet.png").convert_alpha()

ufo_img = pygame.image.load("images/ufo.png").convert_alpha()

explosion_img = pygame.image.load("images/explosion.png").convert_alpha()
```

Load sounds: bg music, fire sound, hit sound

Chapter 7: Simple Shooter

```
pygame.mixer.music.load("audio/bg_music.mp3")
fire_sound = pygame.mixer.Sound("audio/fire.wav")
hit_sound = pygame.mixer.Sound("audio/hit.wav")
```

Play background music in a loop

```
pygame.mixer.music.play(-1)
```

Create Rect for rocket at bottom of screen

```
rocket_rect = rocket_img.get_rect(midbottom=(400, 580))
```

Create Rect for bullet at rocket's nose

```
bullet_rect = bullet_img.get_rect(midbottom=rocket_rect.midtop)
```

Create Rect for UFO near top of screen

```
ufo_rect = ufo_img.get_rect(topleft=(50, 50))
```

Create Rect for explosion (hidden)

```
explosion_rect = explosion_img.get_rect()
```

Set bullet as inactive

```
bullet_active = False
```

Set UFO speed

```
ufo_speed = 5
```

Set explosion timer to zero

```
explosion_timer = 0
explosion_limit = 30   # frames
```

2. GAME LOOP: WHILE game is running

```
running = True
while running:
```

Chapter 7: Simple Shooter

CHECK for events

```
for event in pygame.event.get():
```

IF quit event or Escape key pressed

```
    if event.type == pygame.QUIT:
        running = False
    elif event.type == pygame.KEYDOWN and event.key == pygame.K_ESCAPE:
        running = False
```

IF space bar AND bullet inactive

```
    elif event.type == pygame.KEYDOWN and event.key == pygame.K_SPACE and not bullet_active:
        bullet_rect.midbottom = rocket_rect.midtop
        bullet_active = True
        fire_sound.play()
```

Move rocket left/right

```
keys = pygame.key.get_pressed()
if keys[pygame.K_LEFT]:
    rocket_rect.x -= 5
if keys[pygame.K_RIGHT]:
    rocket_rect.x += 5
```

KEEP rocket inside screen bounds

```
rocket_rect.x = max(0, min(rocket_rect.x, 800 - rocket_rect.width))
```

MOVE UFO horizontally by its speed

```
ufo_rect.x += ufo_speed
```

Chapter 7: Simple Shooter

IF UFO reaches left or right edge, reverse UFO direction

```
if ufo_rect.left <= 0 or ufo_rect.right >= 800:
    ufo_speed = -ufo_speed
```

IF bullet is active

```
if bullet_active:
    bullet_rect.y -= 10
```

IF bullet leaves top of screen, mark bullet as inactive

```
        if bullet_rect.bottom < 0:
            bullet_active = False
```

IF bullet active AND collide with UFO

```
if bullet_active and bullet_rect.
                        colliderect(ufo_rect):
    hit_sound.play()
    explosion_rect.center = ufo_rect.center
    explosion_timer = 0
    bullet_active = False
    bullet_rect.midbottom = rocket_rect.midtop
    ufo_rect.topleft = (50, 50)
```

IF explosion is showing

```
if explosion_timer < explosion_limit:
    explosion_timer += 1
```

CLEAR the screen

```
screen.fill((0, 0, 0))
```

DRAW rocket

```
screen.blit(rocket_img, rocket_rect)
```

Chapter 7: Simple Shooter

DRAW UFO

```
    screen.blit(ufo_img, ufo_rect)
```

IF bullet is active, DRAW bullet

```
    if bullet_active:
        screen.blit(bullet_img, bullet_rect)
```

IF explosion is showing on screen, DRAW explosion

```
    if explosion_timer < explosion_limit:
        screen.blit(explosion_img, explosion_rect)
```

UPDATE display

```
    pygame.display.flip()
    clock.tick(60)
```

3. END Stop background music and close

```
pygame.mixer.music.stop()
pygame.quit()
```

Challenge

You now have a working single-screen shooter — but you can make it more exciting by adding your own features.

Chapter 7: Simple Shooter

Here are some suggestions to try:

1. Fix the error with the explosion showing as the game starts. You want this to only show when the ufo and the bullet collide.

2. Score Counter
   - Create a score variable starting at 0.
   - Increase it every time the UFO is hit.
   - Use pygame.font.Font to display the score in the top-left corner of the screen.

3. Multiple UFO Speeds
   - Each time the UFO is hit, make it respawn moving slightly faster than before.
   - Keep increasing speed until it becomes challenging to hit.

4. Lives System
   - Give the player 3 lives.
   - Lose a life if the UFO reaches the bottom of the screen (you'll need to move it downward after each bounce).
   - End the game when lives reach 0 and show a "Game Over" message.

5. Double Fire Upgrade
   - Allow two bullets on screen at the same time instead of one.
   - This means changing the bullet_fired flag to handle a list of bullets instead of a single one.

6. Background Image
   - Instead of filling the screen with black, load a background image (e.g., images/space.png) and blit it each frame.

7. Make the enemy UFO drop bombs. Player loses a life if hit by bomb.

8 My Invaders Project

In this project, you'll build My Invaders — a retro-style arcade shooter inspired by the 1978 classic "Space Invaders". You'll control a spaceship positioned at the bottom of the screen and shoot upward to defend Earth from rows of advancing alien invaders. The player fires using the space bar, and each projectile moves upward until it either hits an enemy or leaves the screen.

Note that in the printed book, some lines of code may wrap onto multiple lines due to formatting, but in your code editor they should be typed as a single continuous line.

We've included all the source code for this chapter in the projects section of the following repository:

elluminetpress.com/pygames

You'll find the final game code listing as myinvaders.py

Chapter 8: My Invaders Project

Game Description

The player controls a spaceship at the bottom of the screen, moving left and right with the arrow keys. Pressing the spacebar fires bullets upward from the ship.

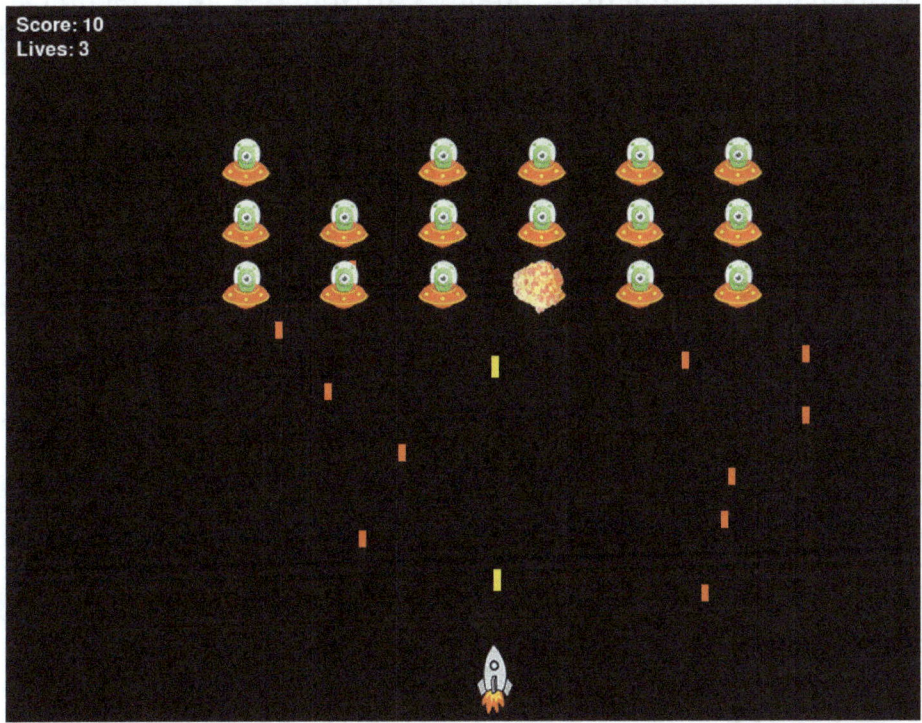

A fleet of enemies moves together horizontally, reversing direction and stepping down when an enemy reaches the left or right edge.

Enemies occasionally drop red bombs at random intervals, which fall straight down toward the player.

If a bomb hits the player, or if enemies descend to the player's row, the player loses a life.

When all lives are lost, the game enters Game Over, where the player can press R to restart.

The player and enemies use image sprites. Bullets and bombs are drawn as simple colored rectangles for clarity and fast collision detection.

Chapter 8: My Invaders Project

Requirements

These are separated into two categories: functional requirements, which describe the specific actions and features the game must perform, and non-functional requirements, which define performance standards, quality attributes, and technical constraints.

By outlining these early, we create a clear target for the design and implementation phases.

Functional

Player moves left and right using arrow keys.

Player fires bullets with the spacebar.

Bullets travel upward and remove enemies on contact.

Enemies are arranged in a grid and move together horizontally.

When any enemy reaches a screen edge, the fleet reverses direction and steps down.

Enemies can drop bombs with a small random chance each frame.

Bombs travel downward and remove one player life on contact.

If any enemy reaches the player's row, the player loses a life.

Game ends when player lives reach zero.

Player can restart with R during Game Over.

Non-Functional

Target resolution: 800×600 pixels.

Frame rate: 60 FPS for smooth motion.

Player and enemy graphics loaded from PNG files.

Bullets (yellow) and bombs (red) use solid rectangle drawing.

Chapter 8: My Invaders Project

Assets

You need the following image files stored in the correct folders so the code can load them successfully. All file names in the code are case-sensitive.

```
myinvaders/
    ├── images/
    │       ├── player.png
    │       ├── enemy.png
    │       └── explosion.png
    └── myinvaders.py
```

Analysis

From the game description, the nouns become our objects, so we have:

- **Player** – Controlled by the user.
- **Bullet** – Fired by the player.
- **Bomb** – Dropped by enemies.
- **Enemy** – A single enemy alien in the fleet.
- **Fleet** – Manages the group of enemies.

The verbs become the responsibilities (actions each object performs which later become the methods).

Player

    Move left/right → moveplayer(keys)

    Fire bullets → shoot()

    Draw player → draw()

Bullet

    Move upward → movebullet()

    Draw bullet → draw()

Chapter 8: My Invaders Project

Bomb

 Move downward → movebomb()

 Draw bomb → draw()

Enemy

 Draw enemy → draw()

Fleet

 Move horizontally and step down → movefleet()

 Drop bombs → drop_bombs()

 Add explosions → add_explosion()

 Draw all enemies and explosions → draw()

Design & Implementation

Now that we know what each object is responsible for, we can decide how those responsibilities will be carried out in code.

Each responsibility will be implemented as a method — an action the object can perform.

We also decide what attributes (or data) each object needs to store so those methods can work.

These attributes are the object's internal variables — they store its position, image, speed, timers, and other values it needs during the game.

So to do this, we turn each of these objects into a class. A class is the blueprint in code that describes what data (attributes) the object will store and what actions (methods) the object can perform.

First is the Player. The player needs to move left and right, shoot bullets, and draw itself on screen.

We also need to position the player at the bottom of the screen.

Chapter 8: My Invaders Project

The Player

The player's ship is the object the user directly controls. It needs to move left and right, shoot bullets, and be drawn on screen. It also needs to be positioned at the bottom of the screen so it's ready for action when the game starts. We can create a class for this.

First the attributes. These go in the __init__() constructor method in the class. We'll give the Player:

- An image so it can be drawn.
- A rect to track position and for collision detection.
- A speed value for movement.
- A cooldown timer to control firing rate.

The methods will be:

- moveplayer(keys) — moves the player based on arrow key input and enforces screen boundaries.
- shoot() — creates a bullet when the cooldown is zero.
- draw() — draws the player's image on screen.

We can implement this as follows.

```
class Player:
    def __init__(self):
        self.image = player_img
        self.rect = self.image.get_rect(midbottom=(400, 580))
        self.speed = 6
        self.cooldown = 0
```

Here we create a method to respond to the keyboard input, so we can move the rocket left and right. The .clamp_ip() method stops the player going off the edges of the screen. We also reduce the cooldown counter each frame so the player can eventually shoot again after firing. This is a frame-based delay between shots.

```
    def moveplayer(self, keys):
        if keys[pygame.K_LEFT]:
            self.rect.x -= self.speed
```

Chapter 8: My Invaders Project

```
if keys[pygame.K_RIGHT]:
    self.rect.x += self.speed
self.rect.clamp_ip(screen.get_rect())
if self.cooldown > 0:
    self.cooldown -= 1
```

Next, we create the method that fires bullets. If the cooldown is zero, it means the player is allowed to shoot. We reset the cooldown to 15 frames (about a quarter of a second at 60 FPS) and return a new Bullet starting at the player's top-centre.

```
def shoot(self):
    if self.cooldown == 0:
        self.cooldown = 15
        return Bullet(self.rect.centerx - 3, self.rect.top)
```

Next, we create the method that draws the player's sprite at its current position on the screen. This simply "blits" (copies) the image onto the game's display surface at the coordinates stored in self.rect.

```
def draw(self):
    screen.blit(self.image, self.rect)
```

The Bullet

The bullet is the projectile fired by the player's ship. It travels straight upward and disappears when it leaves the screen. It also needs a rect object for collision detection with enemies. We can create a class for this.

First the attributes. These go in the __init__() constructor method in the class. We'll give the Bullet:

- A rect to store its position and size for both drawing and collision detection.
- A speed so it knows how fast to move upward.

The methods will be:

- movebullet() — moves the bullet upward each frame and returns True if it is still on screen.

Chapter 8: My Invaders Project

- draw() — draws the bullet on screen as a yellow rectangle.

We can implement this as follows. Here we set up the bullet's rect object at (x, y) with a fixed width of 6 pixels and height of 18 pixels. The speed is negative because moving up in Pygame means decreasing the y position.

```
class Bullet:
    def __init__(self, x, y):
        self.rect = pygame.Rect(x, y, 6, 18)
        self.speed = -8
```

Here we move the bullet upward by adding its speed to its y position each frame. The method returns True if the bullet is still visible on screen (bottom greater than 0) so the game can remove it when it goes off screen.

```
    def movebullet(self):
        self.rect.y += self.speed
        return self.rect.bottom > 0
```

Here we draw the bullet as a yellow rectangle at its current position. This uses Pygame's draw.rect() function rather than an image for simplicity and clarity.

```
    def draw(self):
        pygame.draw.rect(screen, (255, 255, 0), self.rect)
```

The Bomb

The bomb is the projectile dropped by enemies. It falls straight downward and disappears when it leaves the screen. It also needs a rect object for collision detection with the player's ship. We can create a class for this.

First the attributes. These go in the __init__() constructor method in the class. We'll give the Bomb:

- A rect to store its position and size for both drawing and collision detection.
- A speed so it knows how fast to move downward.

The methods will be:

- movebomb() — moves the bomb downward each frame and returns True if it is still on screen.

- draw() — draws the bomb on screen as a red rectangle.

We can implement this as follows. Here we set up the bomb's rect object at (x, y) with a fixed width of 6 pixels and height of 14 pixels. The speed is positive because moving down in Pygame means increasing the y position.

```
class Bomb:
    def __init__(self, x, y):
        self.rect = pygame.Rect(x, y, 6, 14)
        self.speed = 5
```

Here we move the bomb downward by adding its speed to its y position each frame. The method returns True if the bomb is still visible on screen (its top is less than the screen height). If it returns False, the bomb has gone off the bottom of the screen and can be removed from the game.

```
    def movebomb(self):
        self.rect.y += self.speed
        return self.rect.top < HEIGHT
```

Here we draw the bomb as a red rectangle at its current position. This uses Pygame's draw.rect() function rather than an image for simplicity and faster rendering

```
    def draw(self):
        pygame.draw.rect(screen, (255, 0, 0), self.rect)
```

The Enemy

The enemy is a single alien in the invading fleet. Unlike the player, it doesn't move or fire on its own — the fleet manages its movement and bomb-dropping. The enemy's only job is to exist at a position on screen and be drawn every frame.

First the attributes. These are set in the __init__() constructor method:

- image — the sprite used to draw the enemy.

- rect — a rect object storing the enemy's position and size.

Chapter 8: My Invaders Project

This is set using top-left coordinates so we can place enemies in a grid.

The methods will be:

- draw() — draws the enemy's sprite at its current position on the screen.

We can implement this as follows. Here we store the enemy's image in self.image and set its position using self.rect. The topleft argument in get_rect() means the top-left corner of the enemy will be placed at the (x, y) position given when the object is created.

```
class Enemy:
    def __init__(self, x, y):
        self.image = enemy_img
        self.rect = self.image.get_rect(topleft=(x, y))
```

Next, we draw the enemy's image at its current position on the screen. The blit() method copies the image from self.image to the display surface (screen) at the coordinates stored in self.rect.

```
    def draw(self):
        screen.blit(self.image, self.rect)
```

The Fleet

The fleet is the group of all enemies on screen. It's responsible for creating the enemy formation, moving the enemies as a single unit, triggering bomb drops, managing explosion effects, and drawing both enemies and explosions.

First the attributes. These are set in the __init__() constructor method:

- enemies — a list of all Enemy objects in the fleet.
- dir — the current horizontal movement direction of the fleet. 1 means moving right, -1 means moving left.
- explosions — a list of explosion events. Each entry is stored as (x, y, time) where x and y are the explosion's screen position and time is the moment it started.

Chapter 8: My Invaders Project

The methods will be

- movefleet() – Moves all enemies horizontally in the current direction. If any enemy reaches the edge of the screen, reverses direction and moves the whole fleet down. Also removes explosions that have been on screen longer than 300ms.
- drop_bombs() – Randomly spawns bombs from enemies with a small chance each frame.
- add_explosion(x, y) – Adds an explosion event at the given coordinates, recording the start time.
- draw() – Draws all enemies and active explosions to the screen.

We can implement the Fleet class by first defining its attributes inside the __init__ method. The self.enemies attribute will store a list of all enemy objects currently in the fleet. We also set up starting positions for the first enemy using start_x = 100 and start_y = 50. These values determine the top-left position of the first enemy in the formation. To control how far apart each enemy appears, we define spacing_x = 80 for the horizontal gap between enemies in a row and spacing_y = 50 for the vertical gap between rows. These values will later be used when populating the grid of enemies.

```
class Fleet:
    def __init__(self):
        self.enemies = []
        start_x = 100
        start_y = 50
        spacing_x = 80
        spacing_y = 50
```

Here we create the fleet by looping over row (vertical position) and col (horizontal position) to generate a 3×6 grid of enemies.

```
        for row in range(3):
            for col in range(6):
                x = start_x + col * spacing_x
                y = start_y + row * spacing_y
                self.enemies.append(Enemy(x, y))
```

Chapter 8: My Invaders Project

Each enemy's position is calculated by starting from (start_x, start_y) and adding spacing_x for each column and spacing_y for each row. This ensures they are evenly spaced. Each Enemy object is then added to self.enemies for tracking and rendering.

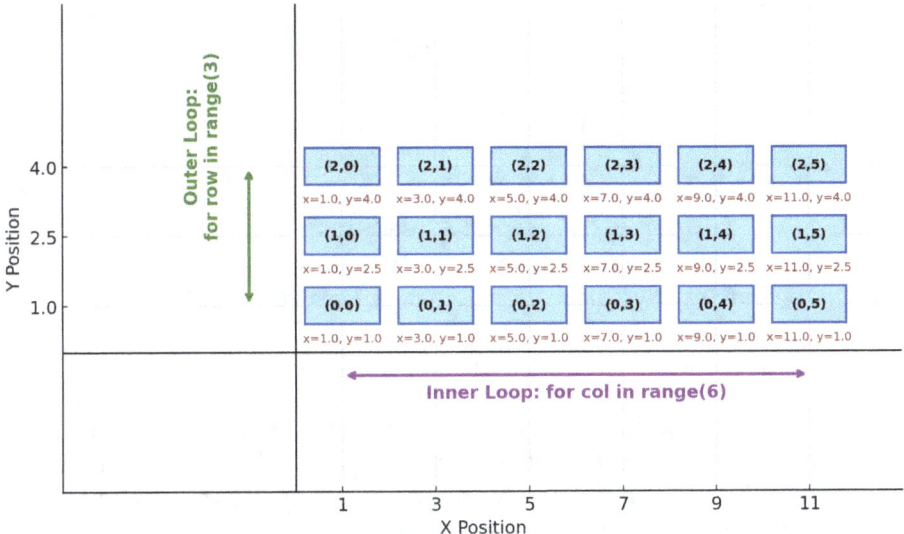

After the loops finish creating all the enemies, the fleet's movement direction (self.dir) is set to 1, meaning it will initially move to the right. The self.explosions list starts out empty because no enemies have been destroyed yet.

```
self.dir = 1
self.explosions = []
```

The movefleet method loops over all enemies, shifting each horizontally by self.dir * 2 pixels per frame. If any enemy reaches the left or right edge of the screen, edge is set to True. When that happens, the fleet reverses direction and moves all enemies down by 20 pixels.

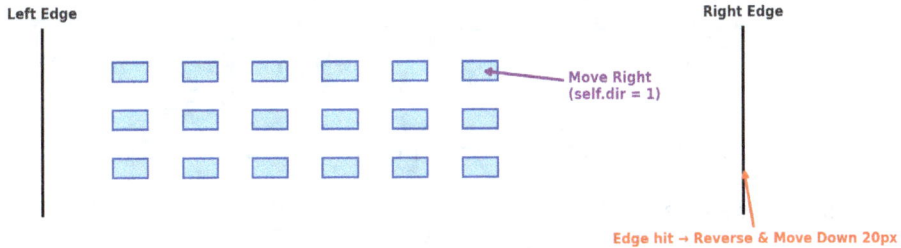

119

Chapter 8: My Invaders Project

The second part removes any explosions older than 300 milliseconds, keeping only recent ones on screen.

```
def movefleet(self):
    edge = False
    for e in self.enemies:
        e.rect.x += self.dir * 2
        if e.rect.right >= 800 or e.rect.left <= 0:
            edge = True
    if edge:
        self.dir *= -1
        for e in self.enemies:
            e.rect.y += 20
    now = pygame.time.get_ticks()
    self.explosions = [(x, y, t) for (x, y, t) in self.explosions if now - t < 300]
```

The method drop_bombs() loops through all enemies and, for each one, has a small probability (0.5% per frame) of dropping a bomb. When a bomb is dropped, it starts from the enemy's centre-bottom position. All bombs created in this frame are returned as a list.

```
def drop_bombs(self):
    bombs_to_drop = []
    for e in self.enemies:
        if random.random() < 0.005:
            bombs_to_drop.append(Bomb(e.rect.centerx, e.rect.bottom))
    return bombs_to_drop
```

When an enemy is destroyed, the add_explosion() method is called with its coordinates. The current time (in milliseconds) is recorded so the explosion can be removed after its display duration ends.

```
def add_explosion(self, x, y):
    self.explosions.append((x, y, pygame.time.
                                    get_ticks()))
```

The draw() method draws all enemies and active explosions.

```
def draw(self):
    for e in self.enemies:
```

Chapter 8: My Invaders Project

```
        e.draw()
    for (x, y, _) in self.explosions:
        rect = explosion_img.get_rect(center=(x, y))
        screen.blit(explosion_img, rect)
```

This first loops through self.enemies to draw each one. Then it loops through self.explosions, calculates the correct position to centre the explosion image, and draws it on screen.

Game State and Main Loop

Before creating the game state, we set up the constants, display, clock, and images that will be used throughout the game.

```
import pygame, random
pygame.init()

# Constants
WIDTH, HEIGHT = 800, 600
FPS = 60

# Set up display and clock
screen = pygame.display.set_mode((WIDTH, HEIGHT))
pygame.display.set_caption("My Invaders")
clock = pygame.time.Clock()

# Load images
player_img = pygame.image.load("images/player.png").convert_alpha()
enemy_img = pygame.image.load("images/enemy.png").convert_alpha()
explosion_img = pygame.image.load("images/explosion.png").convert_alpha()
```

Now that the constants and resources are ready, we create the initial game state.

First we set up the game state, we create one Player object and one Fleet object.

```
player = Player()
fleet = Fleet()
```

Chapter 8: My Invaders Project

We also make empty lists for bullets and bombs because these will appear and disappear during the game.

We store the player's score and lives, and we keep a game_over flag to know when the game should stop running normally.

```
bullets, bombs = [], []
score, lives = 0, 3
game_over = False
```

Finally, we have player_explosion_time to control the short explosion effect when the player is hit.

```
player_explosion_time = 0
```

Next is the main game loop. This loop will keep running until the player quits the game.

```
running = True
while running:
```

We use the clock to make the game run at a fixed speed (60 frames per second), so it looks smooth and consistent on all computers.

```
    clock.tick(60)
```

We also get the current state of the keyboard so we can check which keys are being held down.

```
    keys = pygame.key.get_pressed()
```

This section listens for one-time events such as pressing a key or closing the window.

```
    for event in pygame.event.get():
        if event.type == pygame.QUIT:
            running = False
```

If the player presses the space bar, we ask the Player object to shoot (but only if the game isn't over).

If shoot() returns a new bullet, we add it to the list of bullets.

Chapter 8: My Invaders Project

```
        if event.type == pygame.KEYDOWN:
            if event.key == pygame.K_SPACE and not game_over:
                bullet = player.shoot()
                if bullet:
                    bullets.append(bullet)
```

If the player presses R when the game is over, we reset everything.

```
            if event.key == pygame.K_r and game_over:
                player = Player()
                fleet = Fleet()
                bullets, bombs = [], []
                score = 0
                lives = 3
                game_over = False
                player_explosion_time = 0
```

Pressing Escape or Q quits the game.

```
            if event.key in (pygame.K_ESCAPE, pygame.K_q):
                running = False
```

We only update the game if game_over is False.

```
    if not game_over:
```

Move the player according to the keys being held down.

```
        player.moveplayer(keys)
```

Update bullets — move each one and remove it if it goes off screen.

```
        bullets = [b for b in bullets if b.movebullet()]
```

Update bombs — move each one and remove it if it goes off screen.

```
        bombs = [z for z in bombs if z.movebomb()]
```

Move the fleet and check if it should step down.

```
        fleet.movefleet()
```

Drop bombs — the fleet decides randomly if any enemy should drop one.

123

Chapter 8: My Invaders Project

```
bombs.extend(fleet.drop_bombs())
```

We check every bullet against every enemy to see if they collide. If they do, we remove the bullet, remove the enemy, add an explosion, and give the player points.

```
for b in bullets[:]:
    for e in fleet.enemies[:]:
        if b.rect.colliderect(e.rect):
            bullets.remove(b)
            fleet.enemies.remove(e)
            fleet.add_explosion(e.rect.centerx,
                                e.rect.centery)
            score += 10
            break
```

We check every bomb against the player. If they collide, we remove the bomb, reduce the player's lives, and trigger the explosion effect. If lives reach zero, the game is over.

```
for z in bombs[:]:
    if z.rect.colliderect(player.rect):
        bombs.remove(z)
        lives -= 1
        player_explosion_time = pygame.time.
                                    get_ticks()
        if lives <= 0:
            game_over = True
```

If any enemy gets too close to the bottom of the screen, it counts as a hit on the player.

We reduce lives, trigger an explosion, and check for game over.

```
if any(e.rect.bottom >= 560 for e in fleet.enemies):
    lives -= 1
    player_explosion_time = pygame.time.get_ticks()
    if lives <= 0:
        game_over = True
```

If all enemies are gone and there are no active explosions, we spawn a new Fleet.

```
if not fleet.enemies and not fleet.explosions:
    fleet = Fleet()
```

Chapter 8: My Invaders Project

Before drawing, we fill the screen with a dark colour to clear the previous frame.

```
screen.fill((10, 10, 18))
```

If the player has just been hit, we draw an explosion at their position. Otherwise, we draw the player normally.

```
if pygame.time.get_ticks() - player_explosion_
    time < 300 and player_explosion_time > 0:
    rect = explosion_img.get_rect(center=player.
                                           rect.center)
    screen.blit(explosion_img, rect)
else:
    player.draw()
```

Draw all bullets, bombs, and the fleet.

```
for b in bullets:
    b.draw()
for z in bombs:
    z.draw()
fleet.draw()
```

Display the Score, Lives, and Game Over Text. We use pygame.font.SysFont to draw text onto the screen.

```
font = pygame.font.SysFont(None, 24)
screen.blit(font.render(f"Score: {score}",
            True, (255, 255, 255)), (10, 10))
screen.blit(font.render(f"Lives: {lives}",
            True, (255, 255, 255)), (10, 30))
if game_over:
    screen.blit(font.render("GAME OVER - Press
        R to restart", True, (255, 255, 255)),
                                     (260, 300))
```

Finally, we update the display so all the drawing appears on screen.

```
pygame.display.flip()
```

When the loop ends (because running is set to False), we quit Pygame.

```
pygame.quit()
```

125

9 Simple Platformer

In this chapter, we'll build a simple 2D platformer using Python and Pygame. Platform games are one of the most recognisable genres in video game history, dating back to arcade classics like Donkey Kong, Super Mario, and Manic Miner. They combine precise movement, jumping challenges, enemies, and collectible items.

Note that in the printed book, some lines of code may wrap onto multiple lines due to formatting, but in your code editor they should be typed as a single continuous line.

We've included all the source code for this chapter in the projects section of the following repository:

elluminetpress.com/pygames

You'll find the final game code listing as platformer.py

Chapter 9: Simple Platformer

Game Description

Build a compact side-view platformer where the player runs and jumps across platforms of solid tiles to collect coins while avoiding patrolling enemies. The player moves left and right with the arrow keys and space bar to jump. Coins increase the score when collected. Enemies patrol back and forth. If an enemy touches the player, the player respawns at the start position.

The level is defined using a simple text-based layout, where each symbol corresponds to a type of object in the game. Solid tiles form the platforms and ground (T). Coins (C) are scattered around the map for the player to collect, increasing the score when picked up. Enemies (E) patrol back and forth along platforms, turning around when they hit an obstacle. P represents the player and the dot represents empty space.

```
............
....C...E...
..TTTTT.....
.........C..
...E....TT..
............
....TTT..C..
.P.........C.
TTTTTTTTTTTT
```

127

Chapter 9: Simple Platformer

Requirements

These are separated into two categories: functional requirements, which describe the specific actions and features the game must perform, and non-functional requirements, which define performance standards, quality attributes, and technical constraints.

Functional

Player moves left/right with arrow keys; space bar triggers a jump.

Gravity is applied every frame; collisions with tiles resolve on X and Y.

Coins are collectible; each pickup increases the score by 1.

Enemies patrol horizontally, reversing on tile collision and at the screen edges.

On enemy collision, the player is reset to a safe spawn point.

A simple 4-frame player animation advances while moving and flips when facing left.

Non-Functional

Target resolution: 800×600 pixels; frame rate: 60 FPS.

Tile grid uses 64-pixel tiles; level strings are 12 columns wide to fit comfortably.

PNG assets with alpha for the player frames, tiles, coins, and enemies.

Collision detection uses pygame.Rect for clarity and speed.

Assets

You need the following image files stored in the correct folders so the code can load them successfully. All file names in the code are case-sensitive.

Chapter 9: Simple Platformer

```
simple_platformer/
├── images/
│   ├── frame01.png
│   ├── frame02.png
│   ├── frame03.png
│   ├── frame04.png
│   ├── tile.png
│   ├── coin.png
│   └── enemy.png
└── platformer.py
```

Analysis

From the description, the main nouns become our objects, and their verbs become responsibilities (methods) as we can see in the list below

Tile

draw(surface) – Draw the tile image on the screen at its position.

Coin

draw(surface) – Draw the coin image on the screen at its position.

Enemy

patrol(tile_list) – Move horizontally; reverse direction if colliding with a tile or reaching a screen edge.

draw(surface) – Draw the enemy image on the screen at its position.

Player

jump() – Make the player jump if they are grounded.

move(pressed_keys, tile_list) – Handle input, horizontal/vertical movement, collisions, gravity, and animation.

draw(surface) – Draw the player's current animation frame at its position.

Chapter 9: Simple Platformer

For the attributes, we figure out what information each object needs to store in order to perform its job in the game. Each attribute represents a piece of data that the object keeps track of while the game is running.

Tile

    tile_image – The surface image used to display the tile.

    tile_rect – The tile's position and size in the game world.

Coin

    coin_image – The surface image used to display the coin.

    coin_rect – The coin's position and size in the game world.

Enemy

    enemy_image – The surface image used to display the enemy.

    enemy_rect – The enemy's position and size in the game world.

    horizontal_speed – The enemy's left/right movement speed (pixels per frame).

Player

    player_frames – A list of animation frame images for the player.

    current_frame_index – The index of the current animation frame being displayed.

    player_image – The current animation frame surface used for drawing the player.

    player_rect – The player's position and size in the game world.

    vertical_velocity – The player's upward or downward speed for jumping and falling.

    is_on_ground – Boolean flag; True if the player is standing on a surface.

    animation_counter – Small frame counter controlling how quickly the animation advances while moving.

    facing_direction – The direction the player is facing (1 for right, -1 for left).

Chapter 9: Simple Platformer

Designing the Level

The level layout is defined as a simple text map where each character represents one cell. Each cell has the same dimensions, set by TILE_SIZE, so the layout acts like a grid of equal squares. Screen coordinates increase rightward for x and downward for y.

	0	1	2	3	4	5	6	7	8	9	10	11
0	.	.	.	.	.	.	.	.	.	.	.	.
1	.	.	.	.	.	.	.	.	.	.	.	.
2	.	.	.	.	.	.	.	.	.	.	.	.
3	.	.	.	.	.	.	.	.	.	.	.	.
4	.	.	.	.	.	.	.	.	.	.	.	.
5	.	.	.	.	.	.	.	.	.	.	.	.
6	.	.	.	.	.	.	.	.	.	.	.	.
7	.	.	.	.	.	.	.	.	.	.	.	.
8	.	.	.	.	.	.	.	.	.	.	.	.

Characters in the layout act as symbols:

- T marks a solid tile block
- C marks a coin
- E marks an enemy
- P marks the player's starting position
- . marks an empty space

The layout is read row by row (top to bottom) and column by column (left to right), creating an object for each symbol it encounters.

```
............
....C...E...
..TTTTT.....
.........C..
...E....TT..
............
....TTT..C..
.P.........C.
TTTTTTTTTTTT
```

Chapter 9: Simple Platformer

To place anything on screen, convert its cell to pixels with

`x = column × TILE_SIZE`

`y = row × TILE_SIZE`

This gives the top-left pixel of that cell.

So for example, in the map, the bottom line of 12 Ts is row 8

```
0    ............
1    ....C...E...
2    ..TTTTT.....
3    ..........C..
4    ...E....TT..
5    ............
6    ....TTT..C..
7    .P.........C.
8    TTTTTTTTTTTT
```

Each cell is 64×64 pixels. So, here we are calculating the pixel position of the tiles in the bottom row (which is row 8).

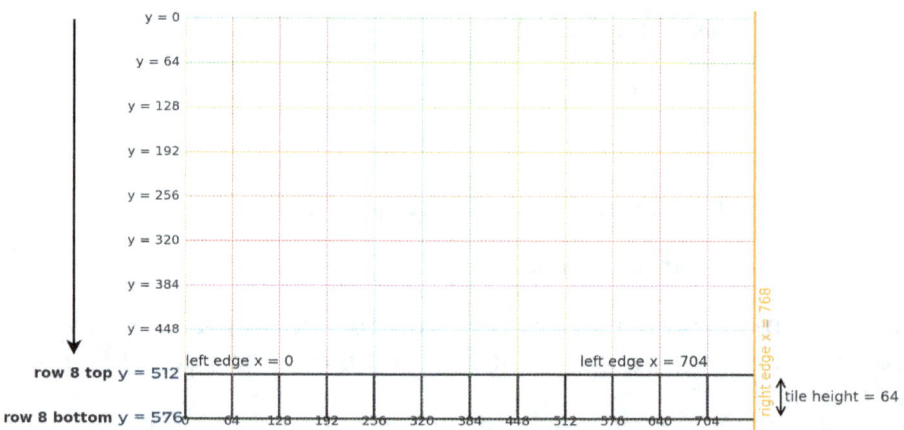

y = row × TILE_SIZE. For row 8: y = 8 × 64 = 512. This means the top edge of the ground row is 512 pixels from the top of the screen.

12 tiles wide (columns 0–11) This row has 12 tiles in a row, starting at column 0 and ending at column 11. So the leftmost tile starts at x = 0 Column 0 means: x = 0 × 64 = 0 pixels from the left edge of the screen.

Chapter 9: Simple Platformer

Rightmost tile ends at x = 0 + 12 × 64 = 768. Since each tile is 64 pixels wide, the last tile's right edge is at pixel 768 from the left of the screen.

Design and Implementation

Now that we know what each object is responsible for, we can plan how to express those responsibilities in code.

Each responsibility becomes a method — an action the object can perform.

To make those methods work, the object needs certain attributes — pieces of data it stores internally, such as position, image, speed, timers, or other values it uses during the game.

So to do this, we turn each of these objects into a class. A class is the blueprint in code that describes what data (attributes) the object will store and what actions (methods) the object can perform.

Tile

We start by declaring the Tile class. A Tile represents the block on the platform. In the constructor method (__init__), tile_image is the image for the tile we pass in when we create the tile object (tile.png). We store it in self.tile_image so it can be drawn later in the Main Game Loop's drawing section, where each tile's draw(screen) method is called to render it on the screen.

```
class Tile:
    def __init__(self, x, y, tile_image):
        self.tile_image = tile_image
```

The next line creates a Rect object positioned at (x, y) with width and height set to TILE_SIZE.

133

Chapter 9: Simple Platformer

This Rect object is used both for positioning and for collision checks against moving objects.

```
self.tile_rect = pygame.Rect(x, y, TILE_
                              SIZE, TILE_SIZE)
```

The draw method draws the tile image at the pixel coordinates stored in the Rect object's topleft attribute.

```
def draw(self, surface):
    surface.blit(self.tile_image, self.tile_
                                    rect.topleft)
```

Coin

Next is the Coin class. A Coin is a collectible that sits inside one cell of the level layout. In the constructor, coin_image is the image we pass in when creating the coin object (coin.png). We store it in self.coin_image so the coin can draw itself in the Main Game Loop's drawing section.

```
class Coin:
    def __init__(self, x, y, coin_image):
        self.coin_image = coin_image
```

The next line creates a Rect object sized to the coin image and positions its center in the middle of the 64×64 cell. We do this by adding half a tile to the cell's top-left pixel (x, y), i.e., (x + 32, y + 32) when TILE_SIZE is 64. Centering this way keeps the coin neatly aligned regardless of the PNG's exact dimensions.

```
        self.coin_rect = self.coin_image.get_rect(
            center=(x + TILE_SIZE // 2, y + TILE_
                                         SIZE // 2)
        )
```

The draw method blits the coin image at the pixel coordinates stored in the Rect object's topleft attribute. Collection — removing the coin and incrementing the score — is handled in the Main Game Loop, in the section where the game checks for collisions between the player and the coin.

```
    def draw(self, surface):
        surface.blit(self.coin_image, self.coin_rect.
                                                topleft)
```

Chapter 9: Simple Platformer

Enemy

Next is the Enemy class. An Enemy patrols horizontally along platforms, reversing direction when it hits a solid tile or the screen edge. It stores an image for drawing, a Rect object for position and collisions, and a small horizontal speed. In the constructor, enemy_image is the image passed in when we create the enemy object (enemy.png). We store it so the enemy can be drawn every frame in the Main Game Loop's drawing section.

```
class Enemy:
    def __init__(self, x, y, enemy_image):
        self.enemy_image = enemy_image
```

Next, we create a Rect object sized to the enemy image and anchor it using midbottom=(x, y). That places the Rect so its feet sit exactly at (x, y). You pass x as the horizontal point you want it to stand on (the center of a cell).

```
        self.enemy_rect = self.enemy_image.get_
                                rect(midbottom=(x, y))
```

Now set the initial horizontal speed in pixels per frame. A positive value moves right; a negative value moves left.

```
        self.horizontal_speed = 2
```

The patrol method moves the enemy's Rect object horizontally by its current speed (2). We move it first, then resolve any collisions.

```
    def patrol(self, tile_list):
        self.enemy_rect.x += self.horizontal_speed
```

After moving horizontally, the Enemy object tests for collisions between itself and solid tiles in tile_list using colliderect(). If it is moving right and a collision is detected, its right edge is aligned with the tile's left edge; if it is moving left, its left edge is aligned with the tile's right edge. This is to prevent overlap. Once the position is corrected, the horizontal direction is reversed by multiplying the speed by -1.

```
        for tile in tile_list:
            if self.enemy_rect.colliderect(tile.
            tile_rect):
                if self.horizontal_speed > 0:
```

Chapter 9: Simple Platformer

```
            self.enemy_rect.right = tile.
                            tile_rect.left
    else:
            self.enemy_rect.left  = tile.
                            tile_rect.right
    self.horizontal_speed *= -1
```

Finally, we clamp the enemy inside the screen. Touching the left edge sets left = 0 and flips direction; touching the right edge sets right = WINDOW_WIDTH and flips again.

```
if self.enemy_rect.left <= 0:
    self.enemy_rect.left = 0
    self.horizontal_speed *= -1
if self.enemy_rect.right >= WINDOW_WIDTH:
    self.enemy_rect.right = WINDOW_WIDTH
    self.horizontal_speed *= -1
```

The draw method blits the enemy image at the pixel coordinates stored in the Rect object's topleft. Detecting contact with the player (and respawning the player) is handled outside this class.

```
def draw(self, surface):
    surface.blit(self.enemy_image, self.enemy_
                                    rect.topleft)
```

Player

Finally we can declare the player class. The Player class is the controllable character: it handles input, horizontal movement, gravity, collisions with solid tiles, facing, and a simple four-frame walking animation. It stores a list of frames, a Rect object for position and collisions, and a few small state variables.

In the constructor, player_frames is the list of images (frame01.png ... frame04.png) passed in when we create the player. We store the list, start on frame index 0, and set player_image to the first frame.

```
class Player:
    def __init__(self, x, y, player_frames):
        self.player_frames = player_frames
        self.current_frame_index = 0
```

Chapter 9: Simple Platformer

```
self.player_image = player_frames[0]
```

Next, we create a Rect object sized to the current image and positions its top-left corner at the starting pixel (x, y). This Rect object is used for both drawing placement and collision checks.

```
self.player_rect = self.player_image.get_
                            rect(topleft=(x, y))
```

These lines initialise movement state. vertical_velocity tracks upward/downward speed (negative is up, positive is down). is_on_ground prevents mid-air jumps. facing_direction controls whether we flip the sprite horizontally. animation_counter paces the walk cycle so it doesn't update every single frame.

```
self.vertical_velocity = 0
self.is_on_ground = False
self.facing_direction = 1
self.animation_counter = 0
```

The jump method applies an upward impulse only if the player is grounded. Setting a negative vertical_velocity moves the player up next frame (screen y increases downward), and we immediately mark the player as airborne.

```
def jump(self):
    if self.is_on_ground:
        self.vertical_velocity = -PLAYER_JUMP_
                                    STRENGTH
        self.is_on_ground = False
```

The move method processes input, movement, collisions, gravity, and animation for one frame. We begin with no horizontal movement.

```
def move(self, pressed_keys, tile_list):
    horizontal_move = 0
```

We read the keyboard state. Pressing the left arrow requests a negative horizontal move and sets facing left; pressing the right arrow requests a positive move and sets facing right. Only the last pressed direction is applied because we overwrite horizontal_move if both are down.

```
self.player_rect.x += horizontal_move
```

137

Chapter 9: Simple Platformer

```
for tile in tile_list:
    if self.player_rect.colliderect(tile.
                                tile_rect):
        if horizontal_move > 0:
            self.player_rect.right = tile.
                                tile_rect.left
        if horizontal_move < 0:
            self.player_rect.left  = tile.
                                tile_rect.right
```

We apply the horizontal move to the player's Rect object, then resolve any overlaps with solid tiles. If we moved right into a tile, we snap the player's right edge to the tile's left. If we moved left, we snap the left edge to the tile's right.

This removes penetration cleanly and prevents corner sticking.

```
self.player_rect.x += horizontal_move
for tile in tile_list:
    if self.player_rect.colliderect(tile.
    tile_rect):
        if horizontal_move > 0:
            self.player_rect.right = tile.
                                tile_rect.left
        if horizontal_move < 0:
            self.player_rect.left  = tile.
                                tile_rect.right
```

We apply gravity by increasing vertical_velocity, clamping it to a terminal speed of 20 pixels per frame for control. Then we move the Rect object vertically and assume we're airborne until proven otherwise.

```
self.vertical_velocity = min(self.vertical_
            velocity + GRAVITY_FORCE, 20)
self.player_rect.y += self.vertical_
                                velocity
self.is_on_ground = False
```

We resolve vertical overlaps. Landing from above snaps the player's bottom to the tile's top, zeros the vertical velocity, and marks the player as grounded. Hitting a ceiling snaps the top to the tile's bottom and zeros the vertical velocity so we don't pass

Chapter 9: Simple Platformer

through.

```
for tile in tile_list:
    if self.player_rect.colliderect(tile.
    tile_rect):
        if self.vertical_velocity > 0:
            self.player_rect.bottom = tile.
                                tile_rect.top
            self.vertical_velocity = 0
            self.is_on_ground = True
        elif self.vertical_velocity < 0:
            self.player_rect.top = tile.
                             tile_rect.bottom
            self.vertical_velocity = 0
```

We only advance the walk cycle while moving horizontally. Every six updates we step to the next frame and wrap around. When idle, we reset to frame zero and clear the counter so the animation restarts cleanly next time the player moves.

```
if horizontal_move != 0:
    self.animation_counter += 1
    if self.animation_counter >= 6:
        self.animation_counter = 0
        self.current_frame_index = (self.
                current_frame_index + 1) %
                len(self.player_frames)
else:
    self.current_frame_index = 0
    self.animation_counter = 0
```

We pick the current animation frame, flip it horizontally if facing left, and store it as player_image for drawing.

```
frame = self.player_frames[self.current_
                                frame_index]
if self.facing_direction == -1:
    frame = pygame.transform.flip(frame,
                                True, False)
self.player_image = frame
```

The draw method blits the chosen player image at the pixel coordinates stored in the Rect object's topleft. This keeps drawing

Chapter 9: Simple Platformer

and collision perfectly aligned.

```
def draw(self, surface):
    surface.blit(self.player_image, self.
                            player_rect.topleft)
```

Game State and Main Loop

Before creating the game state, we set up the constants, display, clock, and images that will be used throughout the game.

```
import pygame
```

This following block defines fixed values used throughout the game. TILE_SIZE, COLS, and ROWS define the grid's dimensions; WINDOW_WIDTH and WINDOW_HEIGHT set the display size; FPS caps the frame rate; GRAVITY_FORCE and TERMINAL_VEL control falling physics; and PLAYER_SPEED and PLAYER_JUMP_STRENGTH control player movement responsiveness - how fast he moves and how high he jumps.

```
TILE_SIZE = 64
COLS, ROWS = 12, 9
WINDOW_WIDTH, WINDOW_HEIGHT = 800, 600
FPS = 60
GRAVITY_FORCE = 1
TERMINAL_VEL = 20
PLAYER_SPEED = 4
PLAYER_JUMP_STRENGTH = 17
```

This next section calculates the playable area's width and height (PLAYFIELD_W, PLAYFIELD_H) from the grid and tile size, then centers it inside the 800×600 window by computing origin offsets (ORIGIN_X, ORIGIN_Y). The PLAYFIELD_RECT stores the playfield's position and size for clamping movement or drawing borders.

```
PLAYFIELD_W = COLS * TILE_SIZE   # 768
PLAYFIELD_H = ROWS * TILE_SIZE   # 576
ORIGIN_X = (WINDOW_WIDTH  - PLAYFIELD_W) // 2
ORIGIN_Y = (WINDOW_HEIGHT - PLAYFIELD_H) // 2
PLAYFIELD_RECT = pygame.Rect(ORIGIN_X, ORIGIN_Y,
PLAYFIELD_W, PLAYFIELD_H)
```

Chapter 9: Simple Platformer

The helper function cell_to_px() converts grid coordinates into exact pixel positions within this centered playfield, ensuring all objects are positioned correctly.

```
def cell_to_px(col, row):
    return ORIGIN_X + col * TILE_SIZE, ORIGIN_Y +
                                    row * TILE_SIZE
```

Next we initialise Pygame's subsystems and create a display window at the specified resolution. We also set the window title (set_caption), and create a Clock object to regulate the frame rate and synchronize updates to the desired FPS.

```
pygame.init()
screen = pygame.display.set_mode((WINDOW_WIDTH,
                                    WINDOW_HEIGHT))
pygame.display.set_caption("Simple Platformer")
clock = pygame.time.Clock()
```

Next, we load all the image assets from the images folder. The player_frames list stores the four animation frames for the player sprite. The convert_alpha() method optimizes the image for faster rendering and retains per-pixel transparency.

```
player_frames = [
    pygame.image.load("images/frame01.png").
                                    convert_alpha(),
    pygame.image.load("images/frame02.png").
                                    convert_alpha(),
    pygame.image.load("images/frame03.png").
                                    convert_alpha(),
    pygame.image.load("images/frame04.png").
                                    convert_alpha(),
]
```

The next variables store the tile, coin, and enemy images.

```
tile_image  = pygame.image.load("images/tile.png").
                                    convert_alpha()
coin_image  = pygame.image.load("images/coin.png").
                                    convert_alpha()
enemy_image = pygame.image.load("images/enemy.png")
                                    .convert_alpha()
```

141

Chapter 9: Simple Platformer

Creating the Game State

We now parse the level layout map and convert it into game objects — specifically, a list of solid tiles, coins, enemies, and a single player instance. This section below defines the level as a list of strings, where each character in the grid represents a different object in the game: "T" for solid tiles, "C" for coins, "E" for enemies, "P" for the player's starting position, and "." for empty space. The layout is read row-by-row and column-by-column to determine where each object should be placed.

```
level_map = [
    "............",
    "....C...E...",
    "..TTTTT.....",
    ".........C..",
    "...E....TT..",
    "............",
    "....TTT..C..",
    ".P........C.",
    "TTTTTTTTTTTT",
]
```

Next, empty lists are created to store instances of Tile, Coin, and Enemy objects once they are placed in the level. The player variable is set to None until the player's starting position is found in the map, and score is initialized to 0 so it can increase as coins are collected.

```
tiles   = []
coins   = []
enemies = []
player  = None
score   = 0
```

This first part of the code below uses a nested loop to scan through the level_map grid. The outer loop calls enumerate(level_map), which returns both the row index (row_idx) and the row string (row). Each row is a string of characters, where every character represents a tile or object in the game. The inner loop uses enumerate(row) to go through each character in that row, giving the column index (col_idx) and the character itself (cell).

Chapter 9: Simple Platformer

This combination of row and column indexes identifies the exact grid position of each cell. The cell_to_px(col_idx, row_idx) function then converts that grid position into pixel coordinates (x, y) so the object can be drawn in the correct location on the screen.

```
for row_idx, row in enumerate(level_map):
    for col_idx, cell in enumerate(row):
        x, y = cell_to_px(col_idx, row_idx)
```

Once the (x, y) pixel position for a cell is known, the code checks the value of the cell character to decide which type of game object to create. If the cell contains "T", it creates a Tile object and adds it to the tiles list. If the cell contains "C", it creates a Coin object and adds it to the coins list. If the cell contains "E", it creates an Enemy object and adds it to the enemies list. If the cell contains "P", it creates the Player object at that position and also stores the coordinates (x, y) in the variable spawn_xy so the player can be respawned at the same location after collisions with enemy.

```
        if cell == "T":
            tiles.append(Tile(x, y, tile_image))
        elif cell == "C":
            coins.append(Coin(x, y, coin_image))
        elif cell == "E":
            enemies.append(Enemy(x, y, enemy_image))
        elif cell == "P":
            player = Player(x, y, player_frames)
            spawn_xy = (x, y)   # store for respawn
```

Any cell containing "." is ignored because it represents empty space.

Main Game Loop

The loop processes input, updates the game state, checks for collisions, and redraws the scene for each frame.

We begin by setting the running flag to True, then start the game loop.

```
running = True
while running:
```

Chapter 9: Simple Platformer

This part of the loop processes all user input and system events. It checks for the window close button or ESC key to exit the game, and calls the player.jump() method when the SPACE key is pressed.

```
for event in pygame.event.get():
    if event.type == pygame.QUIT:
        running = False
    elif event.type == pygame.KEYDOWN:
        if event.key == pygame.K_ESCAPE:
            running = False
        if event.key == pygame.K_SPACE:
            player.jump()
```

After handling discrete events, we read the current keyboard state with pygame.key.get_pressed() so continuous movement (left/right) can be applied to the player..

```
pressed_keys = pygame.key.get_pressed()
```

Next, we call the player object's move() method, passing in the current pressed_keys array and the list of solid tiles. This method handles input, applies movement and gravity, resolves collisions, and updates the animation for the current frame.

```
player.move(pressed_keys, tiles)
```

The for loop below, calls each enemy's patrol() method, passing in the list of solid tiles.

```
for enemy in enemies:
    enemy.patrol(tiles)
```

The next for loop checks whether the player collides with a coin. A copy of the coins list is used so coins can be safely removed from the original list. If a collision is detected, the coin is removed from the coins list and the score is increased by 1, rewarding the player for collecting it (score += 1).

```
for coin in coins[:]:
    if player.player_rect.colliderect(coin.coin_rect):
        coins.remove(coin)
        score += 1
```

Chapter 9: Simple Platformer

This following loop checks for collisions between the player and any enemy. If a collision is detected, the player's rect object is reset to the original spawn_xy position, and the vertical velocity is cleared to stop any movement from the previous frame. The break statement ends the loop immediately after the first collision is handled, avoiding unnecessary checks.

```
for enemy in enemies:
    if player.player_rect.colliderect(enemy.
        enemy_rect):
        player.player_rect.topleft = spawn_xy
        player.vertical_velocity = 0
        break
```

Here we clear the screen with a sky-blue color to remove objects from the previous frame.

```
screen.fill((156, 220, 255))   # background color
```

Below, the first for loop iterates over each tile in the tiles list and calls its draw(screen) method to draw the tiles that form the platforms. The next loop draws all coins so they appear above the tiles, and the third loop draws all enemies.

```
for tile in tiles:
    tile.draw(screen)
for coin in coins:
    coin.draw(screen)
for enemy in enemies:
    enemy.draw(screen)
```

Next, player.draw(screen) draws the controllable character (player).

```
player.draw(screen)
```

Below, the line creates a default font at 36 px size.

```
font = pygame.font.Font(None, 36)
```

The next line renders the score text into a new surface with anti-aliasing enabled (True) and white text color.

```
score_surf = font.render(f"Score: {score}",
                True, (255, 255, 255))
```

Chapter 9: Simple Platformer

The score text surface is then drawn onto the screen at the fixed HUD position (10, 10) near the top-left corner.

```
screen.blit(score_surf, (10, 10))
```

The next line updates the display so the entire frame is shown at once, preventing visual tearing.

```
pygame.display.flip()
```

The clock.tick(FPS) call then pauses just enough to cap the loop at the target frames per second, ensuring consistent animation speed across different hardware

```
clock.tick(FPS)
```

Finally, we close Pygame

```
pygame.quit()
```

Challenge

In this challenge, you will enhance your platformer by adding horizontally and vertically moving platforms that the player can stand on and ride to reach coins, cross gaps, or avoid enemies. This introduces new collision handling, object motion, and level design possibilities.

If the player is standing on top of a moving platform (collision detected from above), the player should move along with the platform by the same amount each frame. This simulates being carried by the platform and prevents the player from "sliding off" as it moves.

Implementation Hints

- Store the platform's image (platform_image), rect object (platform_rect), starting position, ending position, speed, and direction.
- In the update() method, move the rect object along the axis of travel, then check if it has reached or passed the target position. If so, snap it to the target and reverse the direction.

Chapter 9: Simple Platformer

- After resolving vertical collisions between the player and solid tiles, check if the player's feet are aligned with the top of the moving platform. If so, add the platform's horizontal or vertical movement delta to the player's position for that frame.

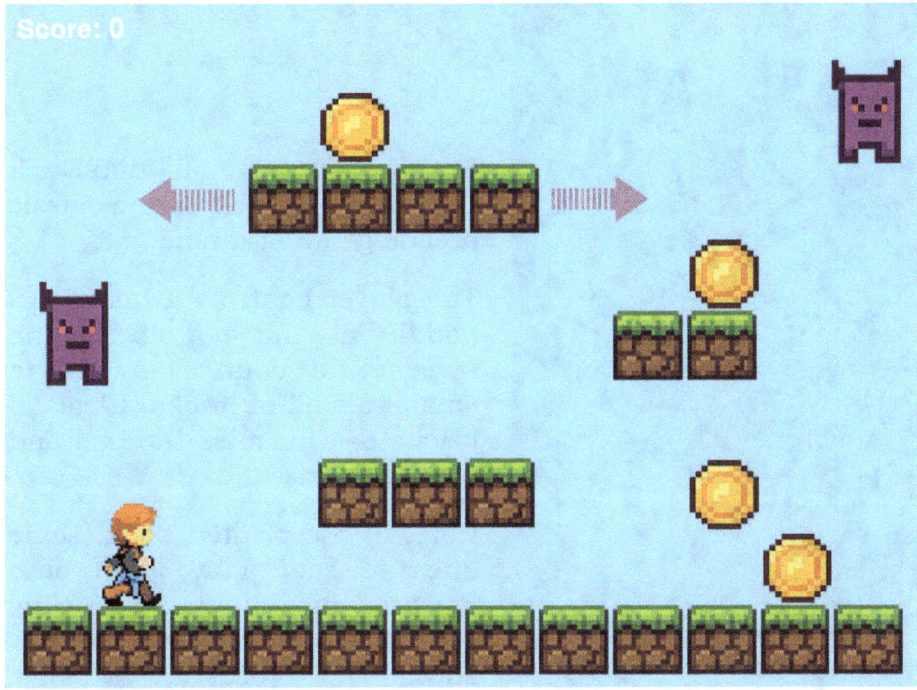

Level Design Ideas

- Place coins or keys so they are only reachable by riding a moving platform.
- Use platforms over hazards (e.g., spikes or pits) to force careful timing.
- Mix horizontal and vertical motion for added challenge.

10

Brick Basher

In this chapter, you'll build Brick Basher — inspired by the classic arcade game Arkanoid.

The player controls a horizontal paddle at the bottom of the screen and bounces a ball to smash a wall of bricks. Clear all bricks to win; miss the ball and you lose a life.

Note, in the printed book, some lines of code may wrap onto multiple lines due to formatting, but in your code editor they should be typed as a single continuous line.

We've included all the source code for this chapter in the projects section of the following repository:

elluminetpress.com/pygames

Chapter 10: Paddle Battle

Game Description

The player moves the paddle left and right with the arrow keys. Press SPACE to launch the ball from the paddle.

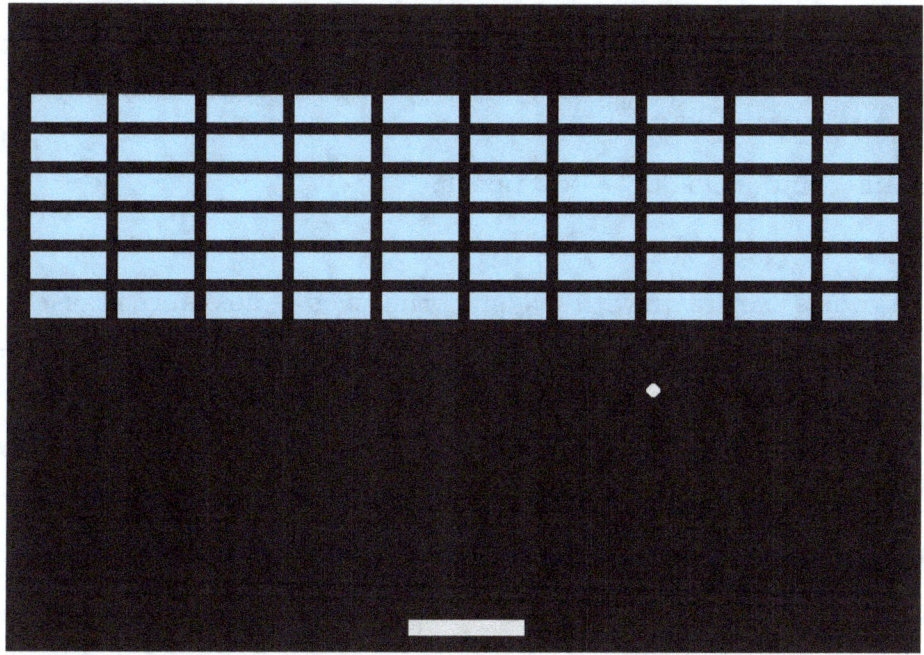

The ball bounces off the paddle, the walls, and the bricks. When it hits a brick, the brick disappears, and the player scores points.

If the ball misses the paddle and falls off the bottom of the screen, it resets on top of the paddle ready to be launched again.

Requirements

As in earlier chapters, we separate functional and non-functional requirements to clarify what the game must do and how it should feel and perform.

Functional

Paddle moves horizontally in response to player input.

Paddle cannot leave the play area.

Chapter 10: Paddle Battle

Ball bounces off walls, bricks and paddle.

Ball removes bricks when hitting them.

Score increases by 10 points per brick destroyed.

Ball resets to the paddle if it leaves the bottom of the screen.

Non-Functional

Game window is 800 × 600 pixels.

Target frame rate is 60 FPS for smooth motion.

Graphics are drawn with Pygame primitives — no external assets are needed.

Analysis

From the description, the main nouns become our objects, and their verbs become responsibilities (methods) as we can see in the list below.

Paddle

> move(pressed_keys, play_area_width) – Read input from keyboard, move horizontally, and keep the paddle inside the play area.
>
> draw(surface) – Draw the paddle rectangle on the screen at its position.

Ball

> reset_position(paddle_rect) – Place the ball on top of the paddle and stop any movement.
>
> launch() – Start the ball moving upward with a slight horizontal push.
>
> move() – Advance the ball by its current velocity each frame.
>
> draw(surface) – Draw the ball (ellipse) on the screen at its position.

Chapter 10: Paddle Battle

Brick

draw(surface) – Draw the brick rectangle (fill + outline) on the screen at its position.

BrickField

draw(surface) – Draw all bricks contained in the field.

For the attributes, we figure out what information each object needs to store in order to perform its job in the game. Each attribute represents a piece of data that the object keeps track of while the game is running.

Paddle

rect – The paddle's position and size as a pygame.Rect.

speed – Horizontal movement speed in pixels per frame.

Ball

rect – The ball's position and size as a pygame.Rect.

vx – The ball's horizontal velocity (pixels per frame).

vy – The ball's vertical velocity (pixels per frame).

on_paddle – Boolean flag; True when the ball is resting on the paddle awaiting launch.

Brick

rect – The brick's position and size as a pygame.Rect.

color – The brick's fill color.

outline – The brick's outline color.

BrickField

bricks – A list of Brick objects that make up the wall.

Chapter 10: Paddle Battle

Design and Implementation

Now that we know what each object is responsible for, we can plan how to express those responsibilities in code.

Each responsibility becomes a method — an action the object can perform.

To make those methods work, the object needs certain attributes — pieces of data it stores internally, such as position, size, color, or speed.

So to do this, we turn each of these objects into a class. A class is the blueprint in code that describes what data (attributes) the object will store and what actions (methods) the object can perform.

Paddle

We start by declaring the Paddle class. A Paddle is the solid bar the player moves left and right along the bottom of the screen. In the constructor (__init__), we create a Rect to store position and size, and a speed value.

```
class Paddle:
    def __init__(self, x, y):
        self.rect = pygame.Rect(x, y, PADDLE_WIDTH,
                                      PADDLE_HEIGHT)
        self.speed = PADDLE_SPEED
```

The move() method takes the pressed key array and the play area width. If the left arrow is held, we subtract from rect.x; if the right arrow is held, we add to rect.x. After moving, we clamp the Rect object so the paddle remains between the two vertical margins.

```
    def move(self, pressed_keys, play_area_width):
        if pressed_keys[pygame.K_LEFT]:
            self.rect.x -= self.speed
        if pressed_keys[pygame.K_RIGHT]:
            self.rect.x += self.speed
        # keep inside play area
        if self.rect.left < MARGIN_X:
```

Chapter 10: Paddle Battle

```
        self.rect.left = MARGIN_X
    if self.rect.right > play_area_width - MARGIN_X:
        self.rect.right = play_area_width - MARGIN_X
```

The draw() method uses a simple filled rectangle to represent the paddle.

```
    def draw(self, surface):
        pygame.draw.rect(surface, COLOR_PADDLE, self.rect)
```

Ball

Next is the Ball class. The Ball stores a Rect for position and two velocity components (vx, vy). It can be in one of two states: resting "on the paddle" awaiting launch, or moving freely. This is the .on_paddle attribute which is true when the ball is on the paddle and false when it's moving freely. When the game starts, we want the ball ready on the paddle, so we initialise this to true.

```
class Ball:
    def __init__(self):
        self.rect = pygame.Rect(0, 0, BALL_SIZE, BALL_SIZE)
        self.vx = 0
        self.vy = 0
        self.on_paddle = True
```

The reset_position() method centres the ball on the paddle's x-coordinate and rests it one pixel above the paddle's top edge. Zeroing both velocity components guarantees it will not drift while waiting to launch.

```
    def reset_position(self, paddle_rect):
        """Place ball on top of paddle and stop it."""
        self.rect.centerx = paddle_rect.centerx
        self.rect.bottom = paddle_rect.top - 1
        self.vx = 0
        self.vy = 0
        self.on_paddle = True
```

The launch() method gives the ball an initial upward velocity with a slight horizontal push so it doesn't travel straight up. move() advances the ball each frame by its velocity. draw() renders the ball as an ellipse.

Chapter 10: Paddle Battle

```
def launch(self):
    self.vx = 5
    self.vy = -BALL_SPEED
    self.on_paddle = False
```

The move() method advances the ball each frame by its velocity.

```
def move(self):
    self.rect.x += self.vx
    self.rect.y += self.vy
```

The draw() method renders the ball as an ellipse.

```
def draw(self, surface):
    pygame.draw.ellipse(surface, COLOR_WHITE, self.rect)
```

Brick

A Brick represents one breakable block in the wall. It stores a Rect for collisions, a fill color, and an outline color.

```
class Brick:
    def __init__(self, x, y, width, height,
        color=COLOR_BRICK, outline=COLOR_LINE):
        self.rect = pygame.Rect(x, y, width, height)
        self.color = color
        self.outline = outline
```

It has a single draw() method to render itself. Bricks are passive: the main loop decides when a brick is removed after a collision.

```
def draw(self, surface):
    pygame.draw.rect(surface, self.color, self.rect)
    pygame.draw.rect(surface, self.outline, self.rect, 2)
```

BrickField

BrickField builds a rectangular wall of equally spaced bricks at the top of the screen. We first compute the available width (window width minus left/right margins), then calculate a uniform brick_width so that BRICK_COLUMNS bricks fit neatly with BRICK_GAP pixels between them.

Chapter 10: Paddle Battle

```
class BrickField:

    def __init__(self, play_area_width):
        self.bricks = []
        area_width = play_area_width - 2 * MARGIN_X
        brick_area_rect = pygame.Rect(MARGIN_X,
        TOP_BRICK_AREA, area_width, BRICK_AREA_
        HEIGHT)
        brick_width = (brick_area_rect.width -
        (BRICK_COLUMNS - 1) * BRICK_GAP) // BRICK_
        COLUMNS
```

We loop over rows and columns to instantiate Brick objects at each position and store them in a list.

```
        for row in range(BRICK_ROWS):
            for col in range(BRICK_COLUMNS):
                x = brick_area_rect.left + col *
                    (brick_width + BRICK_GAP)
                y = brick_area_rect.top + row *
                    (BRICK_HEIGHT + BRICK_GAP)
                self.bricks.append(Brick(x, y,
                brick_width, BRICK_HEIGHT))

    def draw(self, surface):
        for brick in self.bricks:
            brick.draw(surface)
```

Game State

Before creating the game state, we initialise Pygame, set up the window and clock, and create our objects: Paddle, Ball, and BrickField. The score starts at zero. The ball is placed on the paddle ready for launch.

```
screen = pygame.display.set_mode((WINDOW_WIDTH,
WINDOW_HEIGHT))
pygame.display.set_caption("Brick Basher")
clock = pygame.time.Clock()
font = pygame.font.SysFont(None, 28)

paddle = Paddle(WINDOW_WIDTH // 2 - PADDLE_WIDTH // 2,
                WINDOW_HEIGHT - BOTTOM_UI_SPACE - 24)
```

Chapter 10: Paddle Battle

```
ball = Ball()
ball.reset_position(paddle.rect)
bricks = BrickField(WINDOW_WIDTH)

score = 0
running = True
```

Main Game Loop

The loop processes input, updates the game state (including collision rules), draws the frame, and regulates timing.

```
while running:
    # 1) Handle events
    for event in pygame.event.get():
        if event.type == pygame.QUIT:
            running = False
        if event.type == pygame.KEYDOWN and event.key == pygame.K_SPACE and ball.on_paddle:
            ball.launch()
```

To update the paddle, we read the current keyboard state once per frame, then move the paddle and keep it inside the play area.

```
    keys = pygame.key.get_pressed()
    paddle.move(keys, WINDOW_WIDTH)
```

If ball.on_paddle is True, the ball is in its "ready" state before launch, so ball.reset_position(paddle.rect) aligns the ball's centre with the paddle's centre (paddle.rect.centerx) and rests it just above the paddle, ensuring it moves in sync with the paddle and remains stationary until the player presses the launch key. If ball.on_paddle is False, the ball is already in motion. In this case, prev_rect = ball.rect.copy() stores the ball's current position and size so the program can compare its old and new positions later when deciding how to bounce off bricks. Then ball.move() updates the ball's position by adding its velocity values (vx, vy) to its coordinates for this frame.

```
    if ball.on_paddle:
        ball.reset_position(paddle.rect)
    else:
        prev_rect = ball.rect.copy()
```

Chapter 10: Paddle Battle

```
ball.move()
```

We now check whether the ball has hit the walls or ceiling so that we can make it bounce back into the play area. If the ball's left edge goes past the left wall, we snap it back to the wall and reverse its horizontal velocity so it moves right.

```
if ball.rect.left <= MARGIN_X:
    ball.rect.left = MARGIN_X
    ball.vx = -ball.vx
```

If the ball's right edge goes past the right wall, we snap it back to that wall and reverse the horizontal velocity so it moves left.

```
if ball.rect.right >= WINDOW_WIDTH - MARGIN_X:
    ball.rect.right = WINDOW_WIDTH - MARGIN_X
    ball.vx = -ball.vx
```

Finally, if the ball's top edge goes above the ceiling, we snap it down to the ceiling and reverse the vertical velocity so it travels downward again. This keeps the ball inside the play area and ensures the bounces happen smoothly.

```
if ball.rect.top <= MARGIN_X:
    ball.rect.top = MARGIN_X
    ball.vy = -ball.vy
```

We check if the ball's top edge has moved beyond the bottom of the screen, which means it has been missed by the paddle and is lost. If this happens, we call ball.reset_position(paddle.rect) to place it back on top of the paddle, ready for the next launch. This gives the player another chance to continue the game.

```
if ball.rect.top >= WINDOW_HEIGHT:
    ball.reset_position(paddle.rect)
```

We check if the ball collides with the paddle and the ball is moving downward (ball.vy > 0). This ensures we only trigger a bounce when the ball hits the top of the paddle, not when it's moving away. If a collision is detected, we snap the ball's bottom edge to just above the paddle's top to prevent it from sinking into the paddle, and we reverse its vertical velocity to make it bounce upward.

Chapter 10: Paddle Battle

```
if ball.rect.colliderect(paddle.rect) and ball.vy > 0:
    ball.rect.bottom = paddle.rect.top - 1
    ball.vy = -abs(ball.vy)
```

We calculate how far from the paddle's centre the ball has struck by subtracting the paddle's centre x-coordinate from the ball's centre x-coordinate, then dividing by half the paddle's width to get a ratio between -1 (far left) and +1 (far right). We use this ratio to slightly adjust the ball's horizontal velocity, giving the player some control over the rebound angle depending on where the ball hits the paddle. Finally, we check if the absolute horizontal speed is less than 1; if so, we set it to ±1 to prevent the ball from travelling in an almost perfectly vertical path, which would make gameplay predictable and less interesting.

```
offset_ratio = (ball.rect.centerx - paddle.rect.centerx) / (paddle.rect.width / 2)
ball.vx += offset_ratio * 2
if abs(ball.vx) < 1:
    ball.vx = 1 if ball.vx >= 0 else -1
```

In the code below, we check that there are still bricks left in the game. If there are, we build a list of their Rect objects and use collidelist() to see if the ball's Rect object intersects any of them, returning the index of the first collision or -1 if none. If a collision is detected, we remove that brick from the list with pop() and add 10 points to the score. We then work out how far the ball has moved horizontally (dx) and vertically (dy) since the last frame by comparing its current position with prev_rect. If the vertical movement is greater than or equal to the horizontal movement, we treat it as a vertical hit: if the ball was moving down (dy > 0), we snap its bottom edge to just above the brick's top; if it was moving up, we snap its top edge to just below the brick's bottom, then reverse its vertical velocity. Otherwise, we treat it as a horizontal hit: if the ball was moving right, we snap its right edge to just before the brick's left edge; if it was moving left, we snap its left edge to just after the brick's right edge, then reverse its horizontal velocity. This approach ensures the bounce direction matches the side of the brick that was actually hit, keeping the game's physics predictable and fair.

Chapter 10: Paddle Battle

```
            if bricks.bricks:
                rects = [b.rect for b in bricks.bricks]
                hit_index = ball.rect.collidelist(rects)
                if hit_index != -1:
                    hit_brick = bricks.bricks.pop(hit_index)
                    score += 10

                    dx = ball.rect.x - prev_rect.x
                    dy = ball.rect.y - prev_rect.y

                    if abs(dy) >= abs(dx):
                        if dy > 0:
                            ball.rect.bottom = hit_
                            brick.rect.top - 1
                        else:
                            ball.rect.top = hit_brick.
                            rect.bottom + 1
                        ball.vy = -ball.vy
                    else:
                        if dx > 0:
                            ball.rect.right = hit_
                            brick.rect.left - 1
                        else:
                            ball.rect.left = hit_brick.
                            rect.right + 1
                        ball.vx = -ball.vx
```

We clear the background, draw bricks first (so they appear behind), then the paddle and ball, followed by the HUD text. pygame.display.flip() presents the completed frame, and clock.tick(FPS) caps the loop to the target frame rate for smooth motion.

```
        screen.fill(COLOR_BACKGROUND)
        bricks.draw(screen)
        paddle.draw(screen)
        ball.draw(screen)
        score_text = font.render(f"Score: {score}",
                                 True, COLOR_WHITE)
        screen.blit(score_text, (MARGIN_X, WINDOW_
                    HEIGHT - BOTTOM_UI_SPACE + 8))
        pygame.display.flip()
```

Chapter 10: Paddle Battle

The clock.tick(FPS) call then pauses just enough to cap the loop at the target frames per second, ensuring consistent animation speed across different hardware

```
clock.tick(FPS)
```

Finally, we close Pygame

```
pygame.quit()
```

Challenge

Add a lives system to Brick Basher so the player starts with a limited number of lives, loses one when the ball falls off the bottom, and can earn extra lives by scoring enough points. This adds a layer of strategy and tension without altering the core gameplay.

1. Starting Lives

Give the player a fixed number of lives at the start of the game (for example, 3).

Show the current number of lives in the HUD alongside the score.

2. Losing Lives

When the ball misses the paddle and falls off the bottom of the screen, subtract one life.

If there are lives remaining, place the ball back on the paddle ready for relaunch.

If there are no lives left, end the game and display a "Game Over" message with the final score.

3. Gaining Extra Lives

Award an extra life when the player reaches certain score milestones (for example, every 200 points).

Cap the maximum number of lives (for example, 5) so the game cannot continue indefinitely.

Chapter 10: Paddle Battle

Hints

Keep track of both the current number of lives and the next score milestone for an extra life.

Update the HUD each frame so the player always sees their score and remaining lives.

Make sure the extra life reward is applied immediately when the milestone is reached, even if it happens mid-round.

Extension Ideas:

Play a sound effect when a life is gained or lost.

Flash the HUD or change the paddle colour when the player is on their last life.

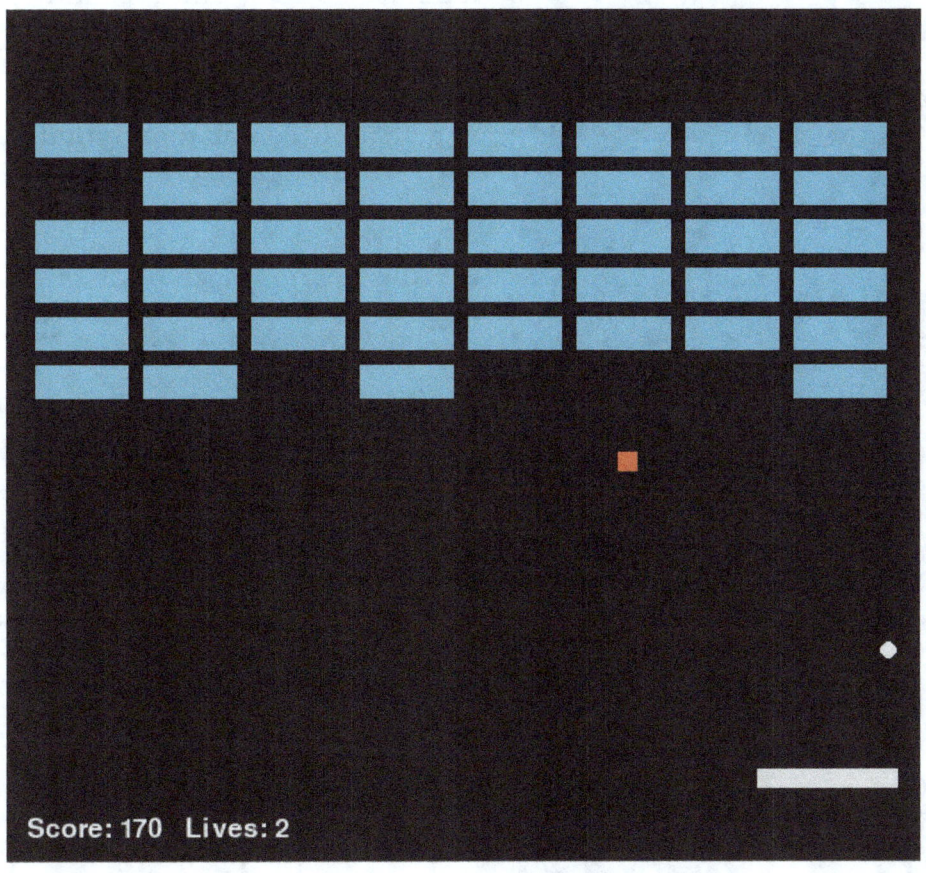

11 Going Beyond Pygame

By now, you have built some 2D games using Pygame, learned how to manage sprites, detect and handle collisions, integrate sound effects and music, animate objects, and respond to user input. You have also applied object-oriented programming principles to organise your code in a structured and maintainable way. These skills form a strong foundation in game development and provide an understanding of the core mechanics that almost every game—regardless of platform or complexity—relies upon.

While Pygame is an excellent starting point for learning the fundamentals, it has limitations that make it unsuitable for large-scale or performance-intensive commercial titles. If your ambition is to move into more sophisticated projects or professional game development, it is worth exploring more advanced engines and frameworks.

Chapter 11: Going Beyond Pygame

Panda3D

For Pygame developers who want to explore 3D game development without leaving the Python language, Panda3D offers a natural progression. This open-source engine was originally developed by Disney for use in commercial titles such as Toontown Online and Pirates of the Caribbean Online, and is now maintained by a Panda3D developer community. It provides real-time 3D rendering, a robust collision detection system, particle effects, and shader support.

Unlike engines with visual editors, Panda3D is entirely code-driven. You write Python scripts to load and position 3D models, apply textures, set up lighting, move the camera, and handle physics and game logic. The engine's scene graph system manages object hierarchies, while its task manager replaces the manual game loop you may be familiar with in Pygame.

Because Panda3D has no built-in level editor, you will usually create models and environments in tools like Blender, then export them in formats such as .gltf, .obj, or Panda's own .bam format for use in your game. The benefit is complete control over every aspect of your workflow—ideal for developers who prefer scripting over drag-and-drop interfaces.

Panda3D runs on Windows, macOS, and Linux, and you can download it for free from the official website.

panda3d.org

Panda3D is a capable Python-based 3D engine, but in 2025 it remains a niche tool with a small community and limited commercial adoption.

It's best suited for hobby projects, educational use, or research where a code-driven workflow is preferred, rather than as a primary engine for breaking into the games industry.

While its niche status means fewer ready-made assets and tutorials compared to larger engines, Panda3D's simplicity and Python integration make it an excellent sandbox for learning 3D concepts. Developers who master it gain a solid understanding of rendering, scene management, and performance optimisation—skills that transfer well to more widely used engines.

Chapter 11: Going Beyond Pygame

Godot

Godot is another open-source engine, but with a very different approach from Panda3D. It comes with a full-featured visual editor for building both 2D and 3D games while still offering a powerful scripting API. Its main language, GDScript, is deliberately designed to resemble Python, which makes transitioning from Pygame relatively painless.

Godot's architecture is built around a scene and node system. Every object—whether it's a sprite, a camera, a physics body, or a light—is a node, and scenes can be composed of multiple nodes to create reusable, modular game elements. This makes complex projects easier to organise and maintain.

The engine provides a rich set of tools:

- Tilemap and Tileset Editors for 2D level design.

- Animation Player for sprite frames, skeletal animation, and blend trees.

- Built-in Physics for both 2D and 3D with collision shapes and rigid bodies.

- Cross-Platform Export to Windows, macOS, Linux, Android, iOS, and HTML5/WebAssembly.

Chapter 11: Going Beyond Pygame

For a Pygame developer, the biggest shift is moving from manual loop and rendering control to Godot's event-driven and scene-based workflow. Much of the engine's low-level work—window management, asset loading, frame updates—is handled automatically, allowing you to focus on gameplay logic.

Godot is free, open-source, and runs on all major desktop platforms. You can download it from the website.

`godotengine.org`

Unity

Unity is one of the most widely used game engines in the world, powering indie hits like Hollow Knight and Cuphead as well as major productions. It supports both 2D and 3D development, offers cross-platform deployment to over 20 targets (including consoles), and integrates with a massive Asset Store where you can purchase or download free models, tools, and scripts.

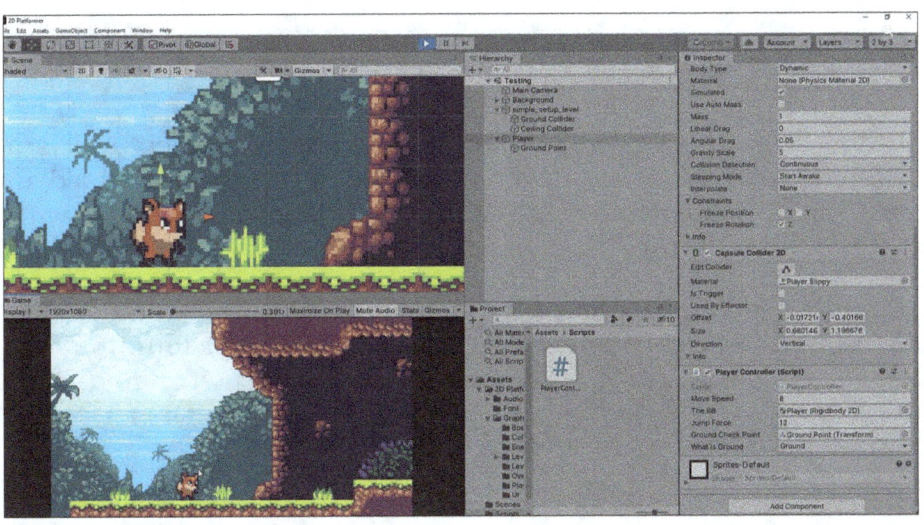

Unity uses C# for scripting, which will require learning a new language if you are coming from Python. However, many concepts from Pygame—such as object updates, collision detection, and event handling—carry over directly. The Unity Editor gives you a comprehensive visual workspace for level design, lighting, animation, and user interfaces, with real-time previews and powerful debugging tools.

Chapter 11: Going Beyond Pygame

Core systems include:

- Physics Engines – Box2D for 2D and NVIDIA PhysX for 3D.

- Rendering Pipelines – URP for mobile and mid-range hardware, HDRP for high-end graphics.

- Animator Controller – Blend trees, inverse kinematics, and complex animation state machines.

- UI System – Canvas-based interface tools for HUDs, menus, and overlays.

Unity is free under the Unity Personal license for developers earning under a certain revenue threshold, with paid tiers for larger projects and studios. It runs on Windows and macOS, with exports available for PC, Mac, Linux, mobile, consoles, and web. You can download it via the Unity Hub from `unity.com`

Unreal Engine

Unreal Engine is known for its cutting-edge graphics and is a mainstay in AAA game development. It is also widely used in film production (virtual sets for The Mandalorian were built with Unreal), architecture, and simulations.

Unreal's renderer supports advanced features such as Nanite virtualised geometry and Lumen real-time global illumination, allowing for incredibly detailed, photorealistic environments.

Unreal offers two main development approaches:

- Blueprints Visual Scripting – A node-based programming system for creating gameplay logic without typing code.

- C++ – Full access to engine systems for high-performance or complex projects.

The engine includes:

- Chaos Physics for destruction, vehicles, and cloth simulation.

Chapter 11: Going Beyond Pygame

- Niagara Particle System for complex visual effects.
- Cinematic Sequencer for in-game cutscenes and camera work.
- Multiplayer Support with built-in replication.

Compared to Pygame, Unreal is a huge leap in scale and capability, requiring you to understand asset pipelines, level streaming, and performance optimisation. The payoff is the ability to produce games and real-time applications at the highest visual and technical standards.

Unreal Engine is free to download and use, with royalties payable only after your project earns above a set revenue threshold. It runs on Windows, macOS, and Linux, with exports for PC, consoles, and mobile. You can download it from

`unrealengine.com`

Choosing Your Next Engine

Your choice of engine should be guided by your personal goals and preferred workflow. If you want to continue using Python while stepping into 3D, Panda3D provides the most seamless transition.

If you value a modern, open-source tool with a built-in visual editor and a Python-like scripting language, Godot is a strong option.

Unity is ideal if you are ready to learn C# and want experience with an industry-standard engine used across the world.

Unreal Engine is best suited for those who aim for the highest-end visuals and cinematic experiences and are prepared for a more complex learning process.

As you develop games in your new engine, it is important to start building a portfolio that showcases your abilities. A portfolio should demonstrate not only the finished products but also the range of skills you possess. Include playable builds, well-documented source code, development notes, and visual assets such as screenshots or gameplay videos.

Video Resources

To help you understand the procedures and concepts explored in this book, we have developed some video lectures, coding demos and resources for you to use, as you work through the book.

As well as the video resources, you'll also find some downloadable files and samples for exercises that appear in the book.

To find the resources, open your web browser and navigate to the following website

```
elluminetpress.com/pygames
```

Do not use a search engine, type the website into the address field at the top of the browser window.

At the beginning of each chapter, you'll find a website that contains the resources for that chapter.

Video Resources

Using the Videos

When you open the link to the video resources, you'll see a thumbnail list at the bottom. Click the images to open the sections.

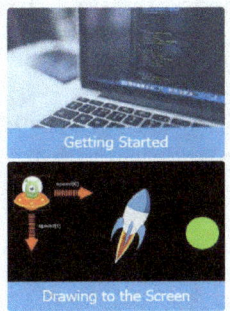  

Click on the thumbnail for the particular video you want to watch. Most videos are between 30 seconds and 2 minutes outlining the procedure, others are a bit longer.

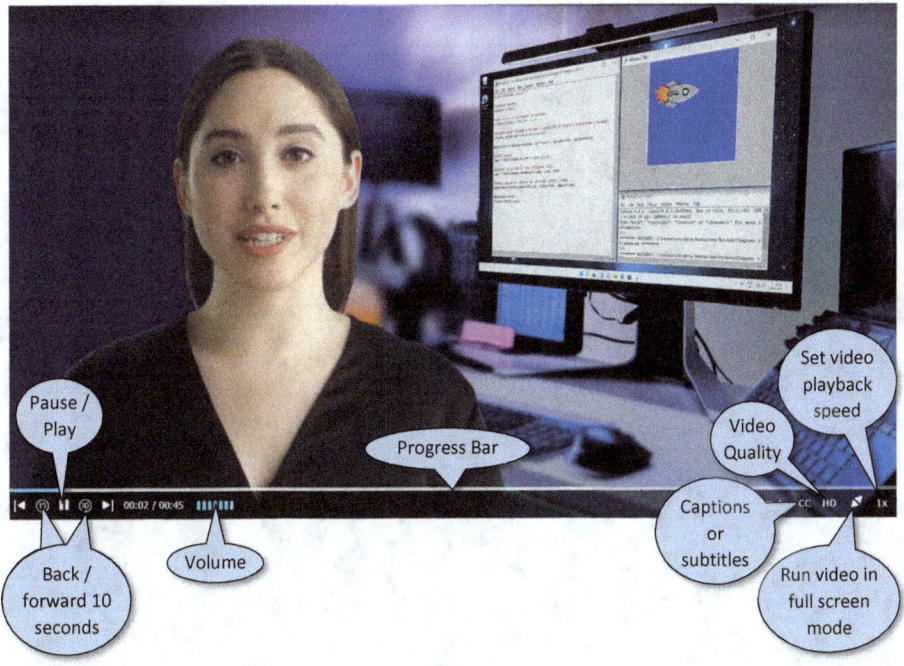

When the video is playing, hover your mouse over the video and you'll see some controls.

169

Video Resources

File Resources

You'll find various cheat sheets, info and code source files in this section.

To save the files into your computer, right click on the icons above and select 'download linked file as'.

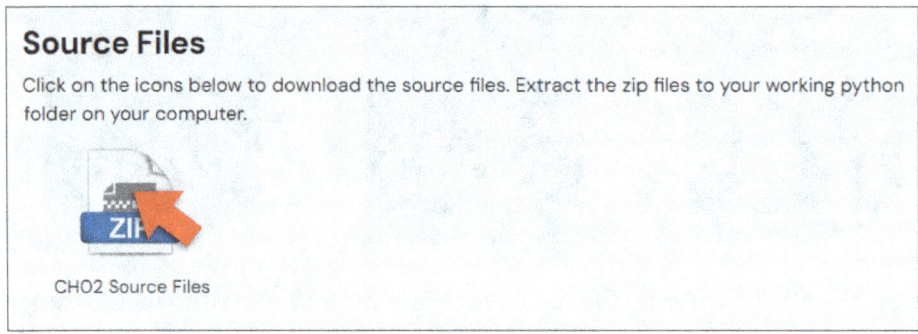

In the dialog box that appears, select the folder you want to save the download into - use 'documents'.

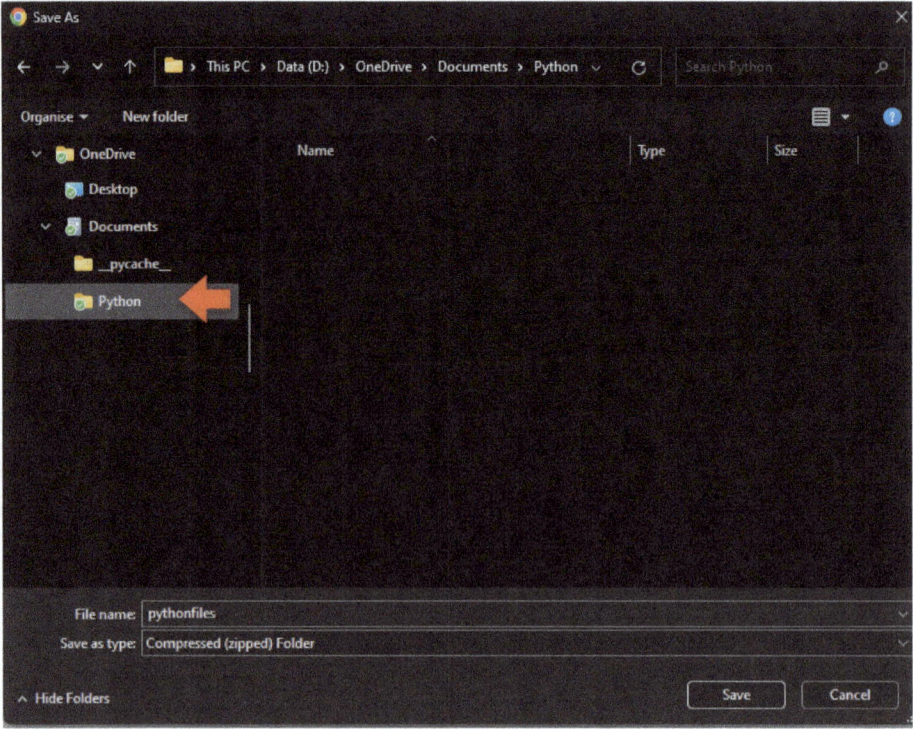

Click 'save'.

Video Resources

Once you have downloaded the file, go to file explorer and navigate to your python folder. Here, you'll find the downloaded files.

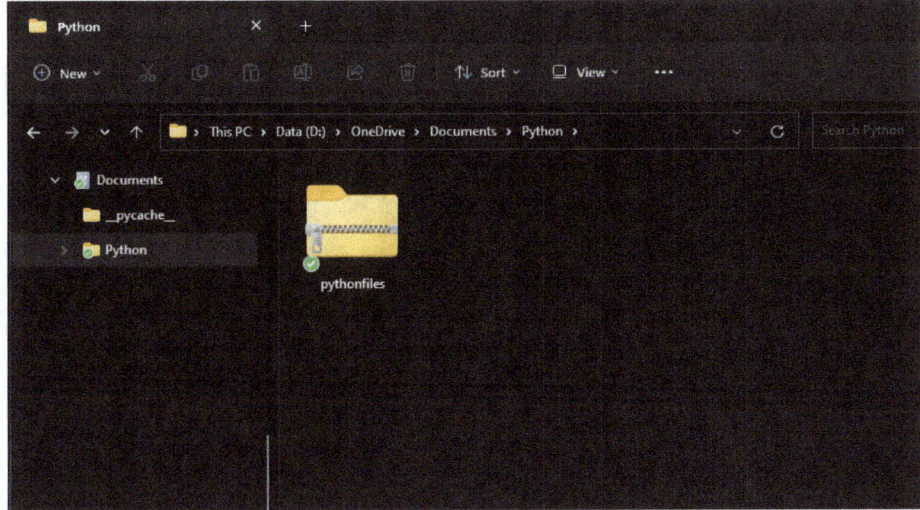

Right click on the zip file, then from the menu select 'extract all'. Then click 'extract'.

You'll also find the source files to the projects. Download these in the same way as before.

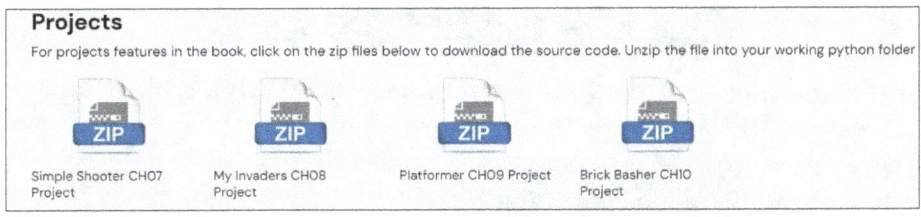

As well as additional bonus projects for you to try. Download these in the same way as before.

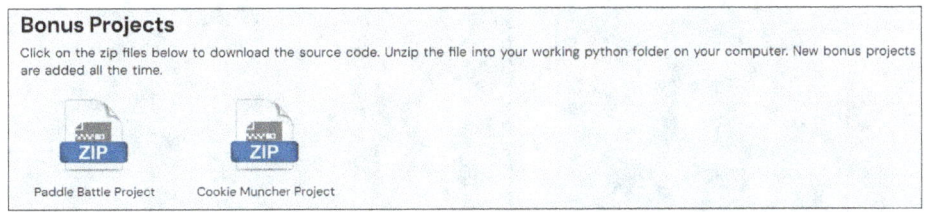

Finally, there is also an online glossary of computing terms.

`elluminetpress.com/glossary/`

Video Resources

Scanning the Codes

Throughout the chapters, you'll find QR codes you can scan with your phone or tablet to access additional resources, files and videos.

iPhone

To scan the code with your iPhone/iPad, open the camera app.

Frame the code in the middle of the screen. Tap on the website popup at the top.

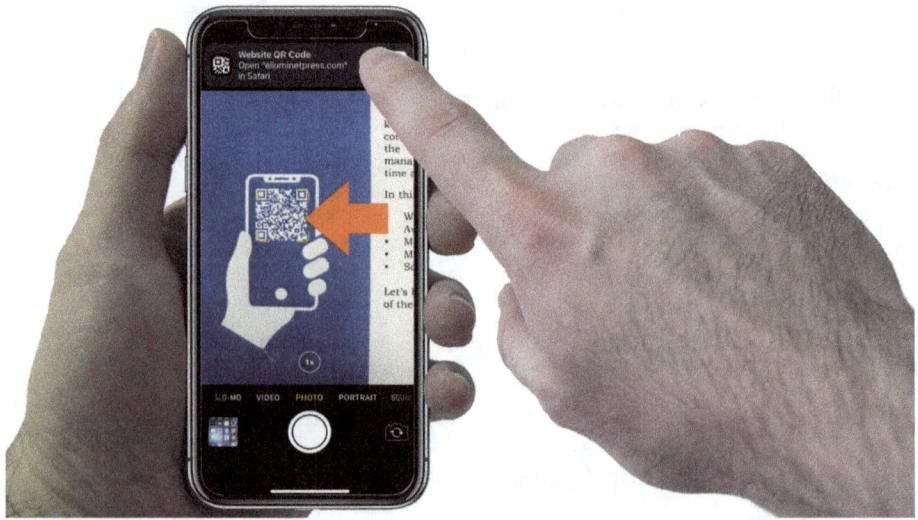

Video Resources

Android

To scan the code with your phone or tablet, open the camera app.

Frame the code in the middle of the screen. Tap on the website popup at the top.

If it doesn't scan, turn on 'Scan QR codes'. To do this, tap the settings icon on the top left. Turn on 'scan QR codes'.

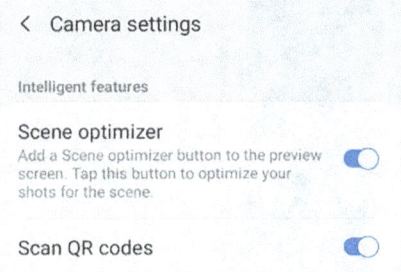

If the setting isn't there, you'll need to download a QR Code scanner. Open the Google Play Store, then search for "QR Code Scanner".

173

Glossary of Terms

This glossary contains definitions for the key technical terms, programming concepts, and game development vocabulary used throughout the book.

Each entry explains the term in the context of Python and Pygame, providing clear, concise descriptions that will help you understand the code, follow the tutorials, and apply these ideas in your own projects.

If you encounter a word or phrase while reading that you're unfamiliar with, refer to this section for a quick explanation.

Glossary

AI (Artificial Intelligence)

Programming logic that enables non-player characters (NPCs) to appear intelligent by making decisions, reacting to events, or adapting to player actions. In simple games, AI may just move enemies left and right, while in more advanced projects it may use pathfinding algorithms like A* to navigate a map. In your Platformer project, enemy patrol behavior is a basic form of AI.

Algorithm

A precise, step-by-step set of instructions designed to solve a problem or perform a task. In games, algorithms may control level generation, bullet movement, collision detection, or scoring systems. A well-designed algorithm is efficient and avoids unnecessary processing.

Alpha Channel

An extra layer in image data that controls transparency. Each pixel's alpha value ranges from 0 (fully transparent) to 255 (fully opaque). In Pygame, images with alpha channels allow for smooth blending of sprites over backgrounds.

Animation Frame

A single still image in a sequence of images used to create an animation. Displaying these frames in rapid succession produces the illusion of movement. A walking character sprite might cycle through four frames repeatedly when moving.

Anti-Aliasing

A rendering technique for smoothing jagged edges on shapes or text. In Pygame, anti-aliasing can be enabled for text with:

```
font.render("Score", True, (255, 255, 255))
```

This improves readability, especially for HUD text.

Glossary

Append

A Python method for adding a new element to the end of a list. Common in games for tracking multiple objects, such as adding bullets to a bullets list:

```
bullets.append(new_bullet)
```

Argument

A value provided to a function or method when it is called. For example:

```
move_player(5, -3)
```

Here, 5 and -3 are arguments that are passed into the function or method.

Array

A structured collection of elements stored in order. Python lists act as arrays for most purposes, but specialized array types can be used for large numerical data. In games, arrays may store level layouts or lists of enemy positions.

Asset

Any external file used by a game, such as images, sounds, music, fonts, or level data. Organized asset management prevents missing file errors and makes game projects easier to maintain.

Assignment Operator

The assignment operator is represented by the equals sign (=) and is used to store a value in a variable or update its contents.

When the operator is used, the expression on the right-hand side is evaluated first, and the result is then stored in the variable on the left-hand side.

For example, this assigns the integer value 10 to the variable score.

```
score = 10
```

Glossary

Python also provides compound assignment operators, such as

```
+=
-=
*=
/=
```

These combine an arithmetic operation with assignment, making it easier to update variables in place. For example, score += 5 increases the value of score by 5 without needing to rewrite score = score + 5.

Attribute

A variable stored in an object that describes one of its properties. For example, a Player object may have attributes like x (position), health (hit points), and speed.

Axis

A reference line in the coordinate system. In Pygame, the X-axis runs horizontally (left to right) and the Y-axis runs vertically (top to bottom), with (0,0) in the top-left.

Background Music

A looping track that plays continuously during gameplay, providing atmosphere. Controlled in Pygame using the pygame.mixer.music module.

Bitmap

An image stored as a grid of colored pixels. Ideal for pixel art and retro-style graphics. Pygame can load bitmap images with pygame.image.load().

Blit

Short for "bit block transfer," blitting is the act of copying one Surface onto another at a specific location. Example:

```
screen.blit(player_image, (100, 200))
```

Glossary

Boolean

A data type with only two possible values: True or False. Often used for conditions like game_over or paused.

Boolean Logic

The process of combining Boolean values with operators like and, or, and not to form complex conditions.

Bounding Box

A rectangular boundary used for collision detection. In Pygame, Rect objects can act as bounding boxes.

Break Statement

A Python keyword that exits the nearest loop immediately, skipping the rest of its iterations.

Buffer

Temporary memory storage for data before it is processed or displayed. Pygame uses a back buffer to prepare frames before they appear on screen.

Bug

A flaw in a game's code that causes unintended behavior, such as a crash or a visual glitch.

Camera (2D)

A simulated viewpoint into the game world that determines what part of the level is displayed.

It is implemented by offsetting draw positions relative to the player.

Glossary

Chaining

A programming technique where multiple methods (or functions that return an object) are called in a single statement, one after the other. Each method in the chain operates on the object returned by the previous method. Often used when working with objects that have methods returning modified copies or the same object For example:

`image.convert_alpha().copy()`

Class

A blueprint for creating objects in Python. Defines attributes (data) and methods (functions) that describe an object's behavior. Examples in your projects include Player, Enemy, and Coin.

Clipping

Restricting drawing operations to a specific rectangular area of the screen. Useful for minimaps, HUDs, or scrollable menus.

Clamping

A process of restricting a numeric value so it stays within a defined minimum and maximum range. If the value is lower than the minimum, it is set to the minimum; if it is higher than the maximum, it is set to the maximum. Clamping is commonly used in games to prevent objects from moving outside boundaries, such as keeping a player's position within the edges of the screen or limiting a character's health to a maximum value.

Collision Detection

The process of determining when two or more game elements overlap. It enables gameplay events such as collecting coins, hitting enemies, or bouncing projectiles. Common 2D methods include bounding boxes, circles, and pixel-perfect checks.

In Pygame, Rect.colliderect() is often used to test for rectangular overlaps.

Glossary

Color Fill

Setting all pixels in a Surface to a single color. In Pygame:

```
surface.fill((R, G, B))
```

Comment

Text in a program ignored by Python, used to explain the code. Written with # at the start of the line.

Compile

The process of converting code into a form the computer can run. Python is interpreted, but .pyc bytecode is created for faster execution.

Constant

A variable intended to remain unchanged throughout a program, often written in uppercase:

SCREEN_WIDTH = 800

Constructor

A special method (__init__) in a Python class that runs when a new object is created, setting initial attribute values.

Coordinate System

A grid used to place objects in the game world. In Pygame, (0, 0) is the top-left corner, X increases to the right, and Y increases downward.

Dictionary

A Python collection of key–value pairs. Useful for storing configuration or game state data. Example:

```
settings = {"volume": 0.8, "fullscreen": True}
```

Glossary

Event

An action detected by Pygame, such as a key press, mouse movement, or quitting the game window.

For loop

A control structure used to repeat a block of code for each item in a sequence, such as a list, string, or range of numbers. In Python, a for loop automatically assigns each item to a loop variable in turn.

```
for coin in coins:
    coin.collect()
```

FPS (Frames Per Second)

The number of times the game redraws the screen each second. Higher FPS means smoother motion.

Function

A reusable block of code that performs a specific task. Functions can take arguments and return values.

Game Loop

The main loop that runs continuously while the game is active, updating game logic and redrawing the screen.

Game State

A variable or set of variables representing the current mode of the game, such as "playing," "paused," or "game over."

HUD (Heads-Up Display)

Overlay graphics showing game information like score, health, or ammo.

Glossary

IDE (Integrated Development Environment)

Software that provides a complete workspace for programming by combining a code editor with tools for debugging, running, and managing projects. An IDE often includes features like syntax highlighting, auto-completion, and integrated version control

Indentation

Spaces or tabs at the start of lines in Python that define code structure. Incorrect indentation causes syntax errors. For example

```
if score > 10:
    print("You win!")   # indented 4 spaces
```

Instance

An individual object created from a class. Multiple instances can exist with different attribute values.

Integer

A whole number without a decimal, such as 42. Used for counts like lives or scores.

Iteration

A single pass through a loop's code block.

Key Binding

Assigning a specific game action to a keyboard key or controller button.

Library

A collection of pre-written code that adds functionality to a program. Pygame is a game development library for Python.

Glossary

List

An ordered collection of items in Python, written in square brackets: [1, 2, 3]

Loop

A control structure that repeats code. Common loops are while and for.

Main Menu

The starting screen of a game, often containing options like "Start Game" and "Settings."

Method

A function defined inside a class that operates on its attributes.

Module

A Python file containing reusable code, which can be imported into other scripts.

Object

An instance of a class, containing both data (attributes) and functions (methods).

OOP (Object-Oriented Programming)

A programming style that organizes code into classes and objects for modularity and reuse.

Parameter

A placeholder variable in a function or method definition that receives an argument when called.

Glossary

Parallax Scrolling

A visual effect where background layers move at different speeds to create depth in 2D games.

Particle Effect

Small visual elements, such as sparks or smoke, used to enhance visuals.

Physics Engine

A system that simulates realistic movement, collisions, and forces.

Pixel

The smallest unit of a digital image.

Platformer

A game genre where the player jumps between platforms while avoiding obstacles.

Pseudocode

A human-readable outline of a program's logic, written before coding.

Rect

A Pygame object representing a rectangle, storing its position and size. Rects are commonly used for placing images, aligning elements, and detecting collisions with methods like colliderect(). They are defined by coordinates (x, y) and dimensions (width, height).

Resolution

The width and height of the game window in pixels.

Glossary

Return Statement

A command that exits a function and sends a value back to the caller.

Runtime

The period during which a program is actively running.

Scope

The region of a program where a variable can be accessed.

Sprite

A 2D image representing a game object.

Surface

A Pygame object representing an image or drawing area.

Tile

A small image used to build larger game levels.

Variable

A named storage location for data that can change during execution.

While Loop

A loop that repeats as long as its condition is True.

```
while player.health > 0:
    player.update()
```

Python Reference

This appendix provides a quick-reference guide to the Python language and the Pygame library as used throughout this book.

It is not intended to replace full documentation but instead serves as a condensed, example-driven summary of the most commonly used features.

Each section begins with an introduction explaining when and why the feature is useful, followed by concise syntax reminders and code samples.

Python Reference

Data Types & Variables

Variables store data your game needs — like player scores, positions, and colors. Python supports various built-in types, each suited to different tasks. Integers (int) – Whole numbers, e.g., score counters, health points, number of lives. Floating-point numbers (float) – Numbers with decimals, e.g., precise positions, movement speed, gravity values.

Type	Example	Use Case
int	score = 42	Scores, counters
float	speed = 3.5	Movement speed, time
str	name = "Alice"	Player names, messages
bool	is_alive = True	Game state flags
list	colors = [red, blue]	Groups of values
dict	stats = {"hp": 100}	Key-value storage

Control Flow (if, for, while)

Control flow statements allow your game to make decisions and repeat actions. Whether checking if the player has lost all lives, looping over enemies, or waiting for user input, these structures define game logic.

If Else

```
if lives <= 0:
    print("Game Over")
else:
    print("Keep playing!")
```

For loop

```
for enemy in enemies:
    enemy.update()
```

While loop

```
while running:
    process_events()
```

Python Reference

Functions

Functions encapsulate reusable blocks of code, reducing repetition and making logic easier to maintain.

```
def move_player(x, y):
    return x + 5, y
x, y = move_player(100, 200)
```

Classes & Objects (OOP)

Object-Oriented Programming (OOP) allows you to group data (attributes) and behavior (methods) into a single structure. In games, OOP is perfect for entities like players, enemies, and bullets.

```
class Player:
    def __init__(self, name):
        self.name = name
        self.score = 0

    def add_score(self, points):
        self.score += points

p1 = Player("Alice")
p1.add_score(50)
```

Game Loop

Every Pygame project runs inside a loop that updates game logic, draws graphics, and processes input. This loop continues until the game ends.

```
running = True
clock = pygame.time.Clock()

while running:
    for event in pygame.event.get():
        if event.type == pygame.QUIT:
            running = False

    screen.fill((0, 0, 0))
    pygame.display.flip()
    clock.tick(60)
```

Python Reference

Drawing & Surfaces

In Pygame, everything visible on screen is drawn onto a Surface. The main screen is a surface, and images or shapes are blitted (copied) onto it.

Fill screen with color

```
screen.fill((255, 255, 255))
```

Draw shapes

```
pygame.draw.rect(screen, (255, 0, 0), (50, 50, 100, 50))
pygame.draw.circle(screen, (0, 0, 255), (200, 150), 40)
```

Load image then Blit (copy) to the screen surface

```
image = pygame.image.load("player.png").convert_alpha()
screen.blit(image, (300, 200))
```

Sprites

Sprites are objects with images that can be updated and drawn automatically.

You use a sprite class in Pygame because it makes managing game objects much easier and more efficient.

```
class Player(pygame.sprite.Sprite):
    def __init__(self, x, y):
        super().__init__()
        self.image = pygame.Surface((40, 40))
        self.image.fill((0, 255, 0))
        self.rect = self.image.get_rect(topleft=(x, y))

    def update(self):
        self.rect.x += 5   # Move right
```

Create player object and add to a group

```
player = Player(100, 100)
all_sprites = pygame.sprite.Group(player)
```

Python Reference

Collision Detection

Collision detection determines when two objects touch or overlap — essential for collecting coins, hitting enemies, or bouncing balls.

```
# Rect vs Rect
if player.rect.colliderect(enemy.rect):
    print("Hit!")

# Sprite vs Group
if pygame.sprite.spritecollide(player, coins, True):
    score += 1
```

Sound & Music

Pygame can play sound effects (Sound) and background music (mixer.music) to enhance the game experience.

```
pygame.mixer.init()
sound = pygame.mixer.Sound("coin.wav")
sound.play()

pygame.mixer.music.load("music.mp3")
pygame.mixer.music.play(-1)   # Loop forever
```

Event Handling

Pygame uses an event queue to process user input like key presses, mouse clicks, and quitting the game.

```
for event in pygame.event.get():
    if event.type == pygame.QUIT:
        running = False
    if event.type == pygame.KEYDOWN:
        if event.key == pygame.K_SPACE:
            print("Space pressed")
```

Keyboard Input

Detecting keyboard input lets players control characters, navigate menus, or trigger actions.

Python Reference

```
keys = pygame.key.get_pressed()
if keys[pygame.K_LEFT]:
    player.rect.x -= 5
if keys[pygame.K_RIGHT]:
    player.rect.x += 5
```

Rect Objects

A Rect stores an object's position and size and is used for drawing areas and collision detection.

```
rect = pygame.Rect(100, 100, 50, 50)
rect.x += 10
if rect.colliderect(other_rect):
    print("Collision!")
```

Colors

Colors are stored as RGB tuples. Values range from 0–255 for red, green, and blue.

```
WHITE = (255, 255, 255)
RED   = (255,   0,   0)
BLUE  = (  0,   0, 255)
```

Fonts

Use Pygame fonts to display scores, labels, and messages.

```
font = pygame.font.Font(None, 36)
text = font.render("Score: 100", True, (255, 255, 255))
screen.blit(text, (10, 10))
```

191

Index

Symbols
- 37
* 37
** 37
// 37
32
% 37
+ 37
< 37
<= 37
!= 37
= 38
== 37
> 37
>= 37

A
and 38
Animations 88
Appending to a File 49
arguments 44
Arithmetic Operators 37
Arrays 34
Assignment Operators 38
Attributes 45

B
Beyond Pygame 162
Blit 63
break 43

C
circle 65
Classes 45, 188
clock.tick 59

Index

colliderect() 84
Collision Detection 84, 190
Colors 69, 191
Comments 31
Comparison Operators 37
Conditional Statements 39
continue 43
Controllers 80
convert_alpha() 82
Coordinates 67
Creating Objects 47

D

Development Environment 22
    Code Editor 22
    IDE 22
    IDLE 25
    Organizing Your Projects 27
    VS Code 23
Dictionaries 35
display.flip() 59
Drawing 189

E

elif 39
ellipse 66
else 39
event.get() 75

F

File Handling 48
file mode 48
float 187
Font 66
Fonts 191
For Loops 42
Functions 43, 188

G

Game Controllers 80
Game Loop 57
Game Window 55
get_pressed() 77
get_rect() 67
Godot 164

Index

I
if Statement 39
image.load 63
Indentation 30
Installing 13
   Windows 13
Install Pygame 21
Integers 187

J
joystick.init() 81
Joysticks 80

K
Keyboard Constants 76
Keyboard Events 75

L
Libraries 51
line 66
Lists 34
Logical Operators 38
Loops 41

M
Match 40
Methods 46
Mixer 93
mixer.init() 93
mode 48
Modules 50
   Built in 50
   Creating your Own 52
Music 92, 94, 190

N
not 38

O
Objects 45, 47, 188
OOP 188
Operators 36
or 38

P
Panda3D 163

Index

Parameters 44
play() 93
print 29
pygame.init() 59
pygame.quit() 59
pygame.time 59

R

Reading from a File 49
rectangle 65
Rect Objects 67, 191
Reserved Words 30
return 45
RGB 70

S

screen.fill 59
set_caption 56
set_mode() 59
Shapes 65
Sound 92, 190
Sound Effects 93
Sprites 72, 189
Statements 29
Surfaces 67, 189
SysFont 66

T

Text 66
topleft 68
Tuples 34

U

Unity 165
Unreal Engine 166

V

Variables 33
Visual Studio Code 23
VS Code 23

W

While Loops 42
Writing to a File 49

SOMETHING NOT COVERED?

We want to create the best possible resources to help you learn and get things done, so if we've missed anything out, then please get in touch using the links below and let us know. Thanks.

 office@elluminetpress.com

 elluminetpress.com/feedback

www.ingramcontent.com/pod-product-compliance
Lightning Source LLC
Chambersburg PA
CBHW052028070526
44584CB00016B/1950